Thomas Shapcott

White Stag of Exile

Allen Lane
Published with the assistance of the
Literature Board of the Australia Council

Copyright © Thomas Shapcott, 1984
First published 1984

Allen Lane
A Division of Penguin Books Australia Ltd
536 King's Road, London SW10 0UH
Penguin Books Australia Ltd,
487 Maroondah Highway, P.O. Box 257
Ringwood, Victoria, 3134, Australia

ISBN 07139 1716 4

Typeset in Times & Frutiger Light by Dovatype, Melbourne
Made and printed in Australia by
The Dominion Press–Hedges & Bell, Victoria

Shapcott, Thomas W. (Thomas William), 1935- .
White stag of exile.

ISBN 07139 1716 4.

I. Title.

A823'.3

for Katalin Forrai
with gratitude

Contents

. . . Mother, mother
don't call me back!
If I were to go back
my antlers would spear you . . .
Each branch of my horns
is a coil of gold rings
each twig of each branch
is a candlestick-cluster
each fang-sharp tip
is a fine funeral candle . . .
I'd dig up my father –
I'd tear off the lid
of his coffin with my teeth . . .
Aiii mother, aiii, aiii mother –
I can't go back to my birthplace now.

(from 'The Boy Changed into a Stag Clamours
at the Gate of Secrets', Ferenc Juhász)

Prelude

Romola Nijinsky at eighty
recalls her family

London. Paris. Vienna. One grows accustomed to the practice of being somewhere. Sometimes I feel I have been everywhere. Other times I feel surrounded by strangers. My apprenticeship was gained within my own family – we took talent for granted, but I could not live with them. I don't think I have ever stopped moving.

My family – did you know my family? You think only of my husband. Poor Vaslav. Everybody does, who has not forgotten him entirely. I dedicated my life to him, but I remained my father's daughter. We have a tradition of restlessness.

Let me tell you something of my own family. Something, first, of my grandfather. His name was Ferenc Pulszky. He was in his time newsworthy: London, Budapest, Vienna. Even America.

My grandfather was a great man in Hungary. He was Kossuth's shadow. You have heard of Lajos Kossuth, the national hero of Hungary? On Kossuth's triumphal tour of the United States in 1851 my grandfather was the one who wrote Kossuth's speech to Congress. Did you know only one other outsider has ever been invited to address their Congress? That was Winston Churchill. I was taught to remember details.

It is not that I want to be considered.

Budapest. Paris. Rome. What I want is some recognition that my own family had meaning. I am not comparing myself with Vaslav. My husband's grace slips into this room, still. You feel it: confess. It is a potential piracy we all practise. I learned that, also. My grandfather, on his American trip, had a witty exchange with Lola Montez, who on the boat set her eyes on the great Kossuth. 'Please, General,' she said, 'the next time you wage war with Austria, do give me a platoon of hussars!' Before Kossuth could say anything, my grandfather promptly replied, 'I am sure, Miss, you would not be satisfied with less.' Most people laugh.

1

All that I play with is offstage gossip. One can make an enduring life of that. One can make endurance.

My father, Károly Pulszky, was a fine man, a famous man. We all called him Charlie.

I hardly knew him. I was a child when he left us. Yet I had a most uncanny knack of seeing his face everywhere. First, in a portrait by Piombo in our National Gallery. It was a portrait my father purchased, shortly before his downfall, so perhaps he saw the likeness also. He was young, trim, enthusiastic. They say he was wonderfully witty and knowledgeable. He was also, like the Piombo, capable of grave apprehensions.

In my later youth I went to London and again in a gallery I saw my father, who had died when I was eight. He was the golden lit saint on horseback in Pisanello's *Vision of St Eustace*, caught in a shaft of forest light. The vision was a stag in that dim and unreal forest. It bears a crucified Christ on its antlers. When I saw that painting I was transfixed. I wept, I had to leave the building. It was like prophecy. My father died in a far-off land, I always thought of it as being in a forest. He sat in a saddle magnificently, I remember that. I remember that.

I forgot to tell you, he was Director of our famous National Gallery. Even the young Berenson was impressed with his collection; after Vienna it was Berenson's first mid-European visit. I believe they both quoted Pater. He seemed a busy, important man, my father.

This was his ring, it came from Egypt. My father was also an archaeologist. A serpent, and a carbuncle gem in the shape of a scarab. Do you find it strange? It is true, yes: sometimes even now I feel surrounded.

But I am not the subject. What was it you wanted to know about my husband and the notorious Diaghilev?

2

The Comtesse Adhéaume de Chevigné in her afternoon salon on the Rue de Miromesnil, Faubourg Saint-Germain, Paris, recounts news received from Misia Sert in Venice

Diaghilev has, it seems, gone to pieces. Or at least, he has been torn to shreds. I mean of course, this news of his beloved Nijinsky's defection. If marriage is not a defection of some kind, I don't know how else to describe it: do you think 'consummate bliss' any less shockin', Princess? But let me read you something of what Misia says about the whole event in its Balzacian splendeurs et misères. She jots it all down with her usual flair for detail and disorder and I am certain she anticipates it will be savoured by us all. You will forgive my lack of a Polish accent as I read her account. What stunning news, though!

'I can see myself entering his room', she writes, 'dangling a parasol, in a dress of white muslin' – only Misia would attempt such virginal felicities – 'Diaghilev was still in his nightshirt, with slippers on his feet ... Performing elephantine capers across the room, in his enthusiasm he seized my parasol and opened it. I stopped playing with a start, and told him to shut it, as it brought bad luck to open it indoors and he was madly superstitious. Barely had I time to utter my warning when somebody knocked at the door. A telegram ... Diaghilev turned livid: the wire announced that Nijinsky was marrying Romola Pulszky, a Hungarian, who had sailed on the same boat to Rio de Janeiro ...'

Romola ... Romola de Pulszky, yes of course I do know her. And no, it is not in connection with the Ballets russes, after all I do not invite every member of the corps de ballet to my house though dear Elisabeth Greffuhle may have suggested as much.

Romola de Pulszky is the daughter of the marvellous Emilia

Markus and of course you've heard of her. No, really? Well, it is not so surprising because she performs only in Hungarian, a language I know nothing of, nor wish to know. Except that I first grew curious to see her act when I heard from Duse that Emilia Markus, as Nora in *The Doll's House*, was preferred by the master, Ibsen, to all other actresses. And from that rigid Norwegian, I assure you this was praise indeed.

Yes, I made the trip to Budapest. The Markus is perhaps the most beautiful woman I have seen. And the final scene! Something shockin' and quite wonderful. You did meet the daughter, Romola? I had her here last season, a confident girl with her mother's ash blonde hair. But as for marriage to Nijinsky. Hmmm. We shall see.

I knew her father, too, a very witty man, dear Charlie. I do not know what happened to him, I believe he died. Did I ever tell you of our larks together? Well, it was some twenty years ago, in Milan, I was quite frisky then. And Charlie was a ball of fun, active as a jack-in-the-box. There was one occasion when I had been to a ball and a party of us decided to call on Charlie Pulszky, to offer him champagne and orange or some such thing for an early breakfast, it must have been 4 a.m. A dozen of us clattered up the stairs to his hotel room, crashed in the door no doubt startling the entire floor of somnolent guests, and then we woke him up by pouring a bottle over his head. He took it wonderfully, dear man.

Except that after we had a sip and quietened down we suddenly had not a thing to say. The joke, you see, had been accomplished, and Charlie had savoured it with such good grace. It was as if he, head to one side, commended it – and us – as a good performance, one he would report back to his wife, no doubt with appropriate embellishments.

This left us all feeling a set of fools – he could have that effect; beneath it all he was a serious young man, a sort of cataloguer. He was, as I recall, also strenuously nervous and I think it was that which infected us. I think it had been only the day before I had been with him at the Scarpa art auction. Indeed, I acted as his 'front' – is that the word, Baron? He desperately wanted a marvellous portrait by Piombo – or was it Rafael? – and we arranged that I should bid for him. He was, d'ye see, Director of the Hungarian National Gallery, and he didn't want that fact disclosed. I enjoyed the bidding prodigiously; things that one does when young and in another country . . .

Perhaps being young and in another country is what made the mysterious Vaslav able to do what it seems he has already done. Nijinsky married? And to the Pulszky daughter? The world moves in tight circles, don't you agree?

But let me read to you just one more paragraph from Misia; I'll not flatter her with more:

'Serge, overcome with a sort of hysteria, ready to go to any extreme, sobbing and shouting, gathered everybody around – Sert, Bakst etc. When the council of war was complete, the terrible event was discussed with greater calm. What had been Nijinsky's state of mind when he left? Did he seem preoccupied? Not at all. Sad? Certainly not. "This is all very silly," interrupted Bakst, "the important thing is to discover if he bought any underpants."'

1894. Budapest

Károly Pulszky writes to his father

My dear papa,

Now that you are at last retired to your estates your absence is sorely missed here in Budapest, though in my imagination I see you surveying the rich acres with a mingled joy and sadness. I will not mention my own boyhood associations with Castle Széchény – the amazement, joy and horror of arriving there with mama from our London exile and my very first view, as a twelve year old, of the Hungarian countryside you both loved. After that long period of absence – my mother had last seen it in 1849, four years before my birth – our return in '65 was to a sadly neglected and desolate shell, and then two years later, her death . . .

But this is a letter of comfort. I took down mama's *Memoirs of a Hungarian Lady* tonight, for some reason. To read to Tessa and Romola. No, to re-read for myself, thinking of you. I sipped a glass of golden tokaji, and opened the book to this page. May its idyll parallel your present enjoyment of life up there:

'On the 31st of October, 1845, we sat enjoying the golden splendour of the transparent grapes, the skin of which is so thin that they cannot be transported without being broken. The rich garlands of vine-branches, brilliant in autumnal magnificence, wonderfully contrasted with the vague outline of the wide view before us, which, covered with the dazzling veil of a hazy atmosphere, gave a dream-like aspect to the boundless plains on the opposite banks of the Tisza.

'Next to us, all was life: – the vintagers, almost as actively eating as gathering the grapes, and but little checked by the presence of the gentlemen, who diligently participated in both these occupations, and smoked no less diligently all the while, – the ladies busy with preparations for the meal, converting the wine-tubs into dinner-tables by covering them with cloths, plates, knives, forks, tumblers, and glasses, and transforming the smaller casks into seats: – the servants bustling and tumbling about, with furs and shawls to be used as carpets: – the vintagers' children lighting luxurious fires, supplied with wood profusely enough for a hundred fire-places. All this offered gay scenes of careless pleasure; but it was not until the dark-featured and silver-haired Márczi, the renowned gipsy leader, appeared with his band, and like a conjurer in a fairy tale, poured forth his charms in strangely expressive sounds, that the genii of joyful merriment seemed to awake.

'Grapes, pipes, cigars, dishes, cloaks, furs, and wood, – everything was forgotten, and old and young danced around in an ecstasy of delight. But the whole effect changed again, as if by enchantment; every face grew solemn, every heart swelled with manifold emotions, when the national Rákoczy March proudly resounded, modulating into the softest expressions of grief at the reminiscences of exalted glory ... Ujhazy, our host, at that time enjoyed with us all the blessings of patriarchal well-being; he is now an exile ...'

No, I will not read on.

Is it possible to recreate joys and moments of bliss once experienced? Or must it be a new venture each time, not a return? I think of you up there, with your new wife. The autumn in Budapest is cold, damp, windy, but I know at the Castle you will be bathed in a clearer, milder light.

For myself, I am so busy I hardly notice the weather outside – unless I go riding, which I do each day now, it is a consuming passion with me, and a much needed release from the pressures of my work.

My work: my joy, rather. It seems all my dreams and plans may yet be fulfilled. The Parliament has accepted my plan for establishing a Museum of Fine Arts.

The Prime Minister, Weherle, as you know, was at once enthusiastic when I presented the concept to him as a major contribution to our national millennium celebrations for '96. That is the key tactic. It is certain the building itself cannot possibly be built by then, but the foundation can be laid – and I (most importantly) have been given a budget of 400,000 florins to enlarge the existing collection. You've no idea the joy that gives me. At last, to have the opportunity to enter thoroughly into my plans to make our gallery one of the prides of Europe. I know the purchases I've managed already have been extolled – the Rembrandts, the Dutch and German masters. But Italy's my goal. I almost feel you by my side in these plans. It was your love of Florence and Venice and the Renaissance that swept me, from childhood, towards that world, as if it were my fate, my destiny. Now I can make it not only mine, and yours, but the legacy of Hungary to have a Gallery of Fine Arts that will become a pilgrimage place for all Europe.

Already there are foreigners who are quite envious. Did I tell you there was a young man – Berenson – from America studying my Italian Renaissance collection. We conversed wonderfully. He has an intuitive grasp of fine aesthetic points, and we discovered a shared passion for Ruskin and Pater. He was at first surprised at my deep knowledge of the English aesthetes (and was a little awed by my perfect command of so many languages – his own English has a sort of American-German inflection, and his Italian hisses like a leaking tube!). But, I tell you, his eye is wonderfully sharp. He looks, he says, for the small betrayals of habit in an artist's work: the ear, for instance, because it is the least expressive detail of a portrait. He tells me he has a massive project of authentication underway. Well, I hope his cunning eye was suitably impressed with what we have. What touched me most was that it was my gallery he must needs survey, after Vienna. I do not quarrel that Vienna's Kunsthistorisches Museum should be his first target outside Italy. But I am quietly endorsed in my secret feeling that it will be our own gallery that will very soon outstrip Vienna in repute and in fineness of judgment. You are aware that Vienna has bought nothing of worth for decades now.

Did I tell you my public talks in the Museum have created enormous fervour? They have been crowded. It confirms my belief that the task of a gallery is not merely to offer fine works and a broad historical prospect; it must also be involved with education and with creating the initial spark of interest so as to waken the whole spectrum of society to their heritage in art. That is why I am delighted to see children being brought in; and my lectures have awakened businessmen, merchants, even shop assistants and servants. To explain with detail, patience and enthusiasm is not to condescend; it is to share, to open, to discover. I swear I, myself, gain most from the experience. It is like the time I wrote my book on national folk design in products of house-industry: suddenly people saw and recognised the treasury of skill, craft and beauty in their most ordinary things: shawls, cloaks, aprons.

One of the special joys in this new support for my Fine Arts Gallery is that old enemies in the Parliament – Géza Polonyi, Károly Várády – have been forced to concede the breadth and vision of my plans. It was approved unanimously.

But that is only the beginning of my task. There is the building itself. That must be impressive enough to invite and exalt those entering. I dream a sort of Parthenon.

But then, inside, the collections must amaze and delight. Art is nothing if it does not broaden our sense of ourselves and of human possibilities. All these things I have laid down, and they will follow – almost of their own accord, if my judgment is right, and I believe quite humbly I have the flair and the judgment (though money, as you know, is a troublesome, messy necessity; I have urged them to provide me with a secretary or treasurer to handle the small change of my buying excursions). Yet this is only the beginning of a larger plan.

I created, years back, the Museum of Applied Arts and Crafts. It stands at one corner of my plan, and reveals the art that can be appreciated in even the most humble artefact.

Then, second, is your own National Museum, and our joint

reorganisation of that will stand for centuries as a model of its kind. It is crowded daily – sufficient tribute.

Third, my Fine Arts Museum – the National Gallery – but even that is only part of the concept. The millennium year forces attention on Hungarian national art and I certainly share your belief that the present time has seen a great flowering. I dream of a special gallery of Hungarian art, with its own perspective and retrospect. I am convinced all flowerings of genius grow from the soil of earlier tests and tribulations. It was you who taught me how to look at and appreciate Italian Primitives.

You see, now, my design? Taken to its ultimate, it would expand to countless museums and places for study of the full range of human effort. Would you laugh if I suggested a Museum of Theatre Art? A Museum of Locomotion and Industrial Art? A Museum of Catering Science?

So. That is just the surface of my present endeavours. My translation of Symons' *The Renaissance in Italy* is almost done, and Emmy urges me to translate our favourite novel, *Romola*. I have recently been designing, myself, her costumes. She is more beautiful than ever, and you've no idea how hard she works on each role. The audience applauds her naturalness and the effortless grace of her movements – each hand gesture is the result of endless study, each small inflection of speech has been pared in the way a sculptor works painfully with stone or wood. I stand in the wings each night – no, not to supervise, to chaperone: to admire and be transported.

Truly, I am lucky to live at this time, in this city, to have this city as my home and centre. It is of a size where I may be expansive and acknowledged, where I may entertain, and where each visitor of note may be introduced and welcomed.

I confess our delight and amusement at new arrivals to our soirées: their amazement and dazzlement at the profusion of fine objects and furnishings in the apartment. It is not a prideful display of indulgence (though some have called it that): it is an offering of the world's munificence, a way to show people the living, lively quality of *things*, and that things are never really inanimate. Things partake of you, just as you partake of their magic, and add your own magic to things. Each rug, each tapestry or chair or marble bust, even each leather book, is a sharing, from one craftsman (or many) to us, and it is the craft I enjoy, and the

9

sharing. Yes, it is enjoyment that binds us to these things, and to each other. If we lose that quality we are done.

I sip my tokaji here and know that you will understand. You understand, also, that our display is least of all some pretence at aristocratic exclusiveness. I am not, in essence, a 'collector'. I like to share. That is a real difference.

I seek a universal art, a universal enjoyment of art, a world where all of life's delights and benefits may be shared. Your humanitarian, liberal principles are mine. In the future democracy of art all men, all women, children also, will join hands and be allowed in.

I hear you laugh, and shake your grey head of hair, and marvel (yet again) at my 'boyish enthusiasm'. So be it. But tonight I am in the mood to believe my good fortune and my future.

I put my mother's book away. It is a book, though, you might read to your new wife – or would that seem cruel? I found myself reading it again with tears streaming.

Sleep well, be well, be happy, dear papa

With love,
Charlie

1895. October 24th. Budapest

Károly Pulszky interrupts a rehearsal at the Hungarian National Theatre of Joszef Kátona's play *Bánk Bán*, in which his wife, Emilia Markus, performs the rôle of Melinda

—Tell her I will not wait until the end of the scene. Do you take me for some telegram boy? How long have you been working on the stage door here? Do as I tell you: go and find Madame Emilia Markus. Say her husband, Károly Pulszky, insists she come this very minute . . .
—But sir. I have strict directions . . .

—Curse of Jove! But she's performed *Bánk Bán* two hundred times! You think she still needs rehearsal? I'll go in myself. You will excuse me, please.

Ah. There you are!

—Charlie! What on earth is all this unseemly noise? It sounded like some messenger or telegram boy. And I wish you wouldn't hurl yourself upon people so. Poor Joszef has strict instructions to allow no one – I say no one – to interrupt my rehearsal, and I'll not have those directions countered.

Now, my dear, what is it? Oh come on, of course I'm not angry with you. Well, calm yourself and tell me all about whatever it is.

—Emmy, if you cannot train these boys to behave in a proper way . . . but never mind. This is important news.

—Oh dear Charlie! I believe you feel just a little miffed. What? Not recognised? In Budapest itself? My dear, poor Joszef can't be expected to know everyone in his first week. You are miffed. Oh come on, dear, I'll get Anna to bring us a coffee in my dressing room. Joszef, inform the producer I'm cancelling the rest of the rehearsal. There, Charlie. You see, I am thoughtful for you. Mari Jaszai will be incensed! See if I care. Now – well, give me your arm – now tell me all your excitements.

—Emmy, Emmy, I would not interrupt your schedule for the world. But it is important. I leave tonight by train. An absolutely exhausting trip. Again. Cologne, Paris, London, Milan, Brussels, return to Paris, Venice, then back to Milan – the Scarpa auction – then Rome and Venice before I return. Which will be after Christmas at the very earliest.

—Charlie! You promised the children this year we would have a proper Christmas, the family all together.

—I know that. Yes I know. But how could I foresee this thing would all work out, and so brilliantly? I tell you, since 8 a.m. I have been a ball of fire, arranging things. There was not a chance even of sending a messenger across to you, which is why I came, myself, as soon as I could possibly slip away.

—Tessa will be heartbroken. And little Romola.

—Oh yes, yes, yes. But they enjoyed an absolutely splendid summer trip to Venice in June. Tessa will not forget that in a rush. Do you recall her face when we gave her the task of presenting a bouquet to Eleanore Duse? And the serenade in the gondola!

11

Really, those girls have had their little share of excitements this year.

Yes thank you Anna, of course, my usual.

So. Now I must tell you the full story. To begin with, the new Minister, Wlassics, called me to his office. He has authorised me to make this second trip, all expenses covered, and he is as keen as I to see we attend the auction in Milan in November. He has given me 122,000 florins – in cash – and I have a free hand. The prize, as I keep telling everyone (everyone, that is, with discretion) is the Piombo *Portrait of a Man*. The one that Moselle still holds to be by Rafael, but it is without doubt by Piombo – I agree with Bode; and, incidentally, that new expert, young Berenson. A stunning work, an absolutely marvellous piece and I will have it. Well. It will demand caution, that is what I dislike about public auctions, the world pokes itself in and you never know what teetering Princess will take a fancy to the very work that you must have. Still, to know that Wlassics is on my side. Thoroughly convinced. The budget for the next three years should be nearly half a million, so I know I can call upon more, in advance, if need be.

—Are you certain of that? Charlie? You know money runs through your hands.

—I tell you, Wlassics cannot wait to secure for the new national collection the very best that there is to offer. And as I pointed out to him, London and Berlin are not buying just now. The time is perfect. At the Scarpa auction there are one or two others that I hope to snaffle, also. A hundred and twenty-two might not last long if I really get carried away. Well, there's nothing in writing, but it's clearly understood on both sides that I have a free hand. The new Government made it quite plain that they want the Gallery to be the very best, and I am the one to achieve that. How could they possibly object if I buy when the buying's right?

—I merely noted . . .

—Emilia, my own, you know better than anyone how a raised eyebrow can be eloquent. But I will not be upset, I'll not allow myself the luxury of that. Besides, there is talk that I may have a secretary to look after the petty receipts and dockets. And of course I allow that would be a most heartfelt relief – I do emphatically not enjoy the bookkeeper's eyeshade and stool myself. But

12

there we are. With Wlassics on my side the whole Government must stand by him – and me. With the change in Government the other week I must say I was under some strain. The Liberals knew where they stood, and of course to have a brother who was Secretary of State. Still, Wlassics is a good man. Indeed, none better. He understood the urgency of striking while the prize is unattended . . .

—But these other cities? Really, Charlie, you impose upon yourself again. I don't know how you can keep it up, this endless, relentless travel.

—My last trip, in June, only paved the way for a whole series of purchases. I am continually amazed, dear Emmy, the way you fail to realize how art works must be coaxed, lured, baited, cajoled, sniffed out and trapped by guile and absolute persistence. Indeed, that is a sort of theatre. Dealers not only have to be deceived and duped – you pretend interest in one painting – that! – while really it is the other behind it you must have. A high first bid, and you'll never gain a foothold further, or at least a foothold worth the price. I have been holding out for things – there's a Weenix, *Family with Rabbit*, a fine Dutch genre piece, that old Glisenti is holding; I've been there three times and merely glanced at it. This trip I'll make my play. And Resimini has a Saint Jeremiah. And these are only Italy, mind you. In London, Colnaghé has a clutch of artefacts that I swear I'll snaffle from him. You've got to play a hard game with these types . . .

—Well, of course we will all miss you furiously. Tessa will be desolate.

—Of course, of course. But think of the gains. You must keep them up to their studies. Tessa's singing is really quite excellent, such a pure tone, you should find time out of rehearsals to listen to her. I'll bring back something. I'll bring you all something. When I am gone, they simply must rely more on themselves.

—We do. We do.

—Did you hear Tessa last night? She was in a wonderful, zany mood. No, of course not, you were at your performance. When I told her that a distant cousin of mine, who was Prince of Madagascar, had died, Tessa strutted around the room like a queen. 'Then I will assume the title', she crowed. 'From henceforth, I am Princess of Madagascar, and will be addressed as such.' That girl really does have her head up in the clouds.

13

—And Romola? Did little Romola curtsey to her? Did she join in the masquerade?

—It was no masquerade. I believe she really meant it.

—Oh, how delicious. We have a princess in the family!

—To me, they both are princesses. Of the most royal blood. Well. This does mean a cancellation of the soirée we had planned for Thursday week. I had a marvellous idea, too, for the menu. Every item would be a pun. The salad would be 'Tsálady' (you remember him?), the fish called 'Fischer'; I had it all worked out.

—Tantalising! Let me help you. When you return we must indeed have our *friendly* menu. Let me think of names. How could we fit in Mari Jaszai? Is there some wine that sounds like? Or a cheese? Yes, a nice rank cheese, would Mari turn up her nose at that? You think, Charlie?

—Dear, dear Emmy. You have a wicked humour. Well, there we will have to leave it. At least for now. Did you know I read a fascinating thing last night? In Java, in the Spice Islands, they classify five senses: these are, seeing, hearing, feeling, smelling – and talking.

—There you are! You must go to Java, or the lands beyond Asia. Perhaps, with your capacity for talking, you would be construed a deity. A god of the senses. And, my very dear, that is exactly how I construe you.

'... For what is that grosser, narrower light by which men behold merely the petty scene around them, compared with that far-stretching lasting light which spreads over centuries of thought, and over the life of nations, and makes clear to us the minds of the immortals who have reaped the great harvest and left us to glean their furrows? For me, Romola, even when I could see, it was with the great dead that I lived; while the living often seemed to me mere spectres – shadows dispossessed of true feeling and intelligence ... I have returned from the converse of the streets as from a forgotten dream ...'

(from *Romola*, George Eliot)

On the *Avon* to Rio de Janeiro

'Nijinsky was half leaning against the railing, in "smoking", holding a small black fan which was ornamented with one gold painted rose. He was rapidly fanning himself. He looked so strange. His eyes were half closed and oh! so slanted ... Suddenly every thought deserted me. I felt a chaos of emotion, saw nothing and nobody any more except the dark, graceful silhouette of Nijinsky and his fascinating eyes. I suddenly heard myself speaking. "Je veux vous remercier que vous avez élevé la danse à la hauteur des autres arts." Kovalevska translated. He did not move. Suddenly he looked at the small ring I wore. I followed his gaze, and, pulling it off my finger, I passed it to him, explaining: "My father brought it from Egypt; it is a talisman supposed to bring luck. My mother gave it to me as I left with the Russian Ballet." It was a green-gold serpent whose head was crushed by a scarab. It had a strange design. Nijinsky held it for one moment and then put it on my finger, saying in Polish, "It will bring you happiness, surely." ... Then I began to talk in French, choosing the easiest words about dance, music, and Wagner, whose work I idolised: Lohengrin, Valkyrie, Tristan, Bayreuth, and my childhood days, which I had spent with my sister and brother-in-law at the Wahnfried at the rehearsals in the Festspielhaus.

'... "Come, come and look at the new constellations, the stars which cannot be seen on the northern hemisphere." We looked up and saw in all its brilliant splendour the Southern Cross.'

(from *Nijinsky*, Romola Nijinsky-Pulszky)

Emilia Markus receives news of her husband, Károly Pulszky

Poor Charlie, well he's somewhere no doubt. Yes, Australia. But where is that?

I doubt he manicures his nails with such fastidious irritation, though he may for all I know. He'll have nothing to collect, there.

How would he, I wonder, live without his prizes, his little discoveries in forgotten vestries, his art collections, his calf-bound first editions? Like his English aesthetes, poor Charlie was at home only in an unfinished gallery. He declared ecstasy in a cracked jug or some quite rigid face daubed on wormy wood. Once I believed that.

Once I admired his flair for digging out old masters. We honeymooned in Italy – where he spent his time in a friar's cassock, deceiving parish clerks and gathering mouldy ikons. I do not go into those galleries in the Museum of Fine Arts, not any more.

I was quite impressed, once, with his authority. That boyish enthusiasm. Enthusiasm is an uncomfortable scholarship, but the past always promised him authority. Work is the only authority. It was he taught me that. Poor Charlie.

In those first years of marriage he read me that English novel, *Romola*. Yes, that is of course where our youngest acquired her name. Each morning over sweet coffee another chapter. He was eager to teach me English, and he did. I think he intended me as a sort of Secretary.

No. I must be generous. He taught me everything. He taught me conversation, his circle of friends, the rapid shift and the shiftlessness in politics. He taught me how to distinguish Tuscan from Venetian costume of the Renaissance. He did not teach me endurance – I think I was born equipped with that, as with my few other fair qualities. His *Romola* translation was published last year, perforce under a nom de plume: Béla Pátáki. He saw that as such a defeat. 'To have lost even my name!', he wept. 'Now I have nothing.' I offered sympathy and advice: 'You should adopt a new rôle', something like that. It was the first time I smelt the deer-odour of failure on him. He agreed with me and left the room.

But there is our good acquaintance, Károly Ferenczy; now he is a true artist. He lives through his work. My Károly was, I think, repulsed by the smell of new oil and raw canvas. He once whispered that Ferenczy should apply varnish, that to work so thickly with brush and palette only implied 'an amateur concern with the future'. Charlie of course, always the Banker, the Investor, the Dealer. Other men's wares. He could spend weeks examining a foxed engraving or a much restored church panel as if God still dwelt therein.

16

Ferenczy paints the light of Hungary on bodies you could hold. Immortal enough for me, friends almost. *Look*, he is saying, and I become riveted. They are immediate.

Charlie patronised him and his studio at Szentendre but budgeted for more Italian Primitives. Somehow, in his eyes, even Ferenczy's work was slotted into a phase, a genre. I think he had his budgets. It was Charlie who first introduced me to Ferenczy. My Károly lived through his work.

Art is a cutting tool that demands complete subjection and offers nothing more than the self can possibly inhabit. Charlie was a fine collector. He sought in his spouse something more than just a toy, a pretty composition to mirror his tastes. He called me his 'muse', and lavished a connoisseur's tributes. It was not flattery. Rather, a form of dependence. He took to wife the one manipulator of mirrors who learned that art is crueller than glass.

My husband cringed, finally, at my appetite. I give; I do not collect. I take; but I take to give back. What I have taken is impossible to justify except that the gift, new-made, returns the hurt as treasure. No, I am not vain about this. I know my value. I am the greatest actress in Hungary.

Sometimes Mari Jaszai is the greatest actress. I stretch myself against her and what I learn returns, refraction. My career has hardly begun. Charlie once wept at my feet. His demonstration was pleasurable, and he thought so too. But I returned to the theatre the next night and the next night and the next. The tears were never personal. Art has not gulped me whole though it is always taking me as if it were pride or anger. It is always surprise. Yes, yes, it was Charlie who first taught me that.

He was generous in supporting me. He shone, he was refracted. In the first years it was like a party, that brilliance. We stuffed ourselves with a life of parties and declared the world must be made to continue like this forever. It was a time when he was most estranged from his father, who declared only that perhaps if we had a child it might impose a new perspective.

My Charlie tugs at the skirts, he wears my ring red sore on this finger but I shall never take it off. I must feel it. I must keep on feeling. Sometimes I feel like a sheet left out in the ice and would crack into pieces at the first hard grip.

They say the Comtesse de Chevigné indulged him. They say his mistress was a 'consolation'. They say he was obsessed by Italy and by me. They say he taught me everything, they say he taught me nothing. They say he was a monster of self-indulgence. They say he indulged me. He indulged me.

They say he thrived in the world of shady dealers and dealt badly. They said he escaped punishment for his offences because of family. They never proved those offences to be more than trivial. I despised them, all of them. They proved how easily viciousness subverts judgment. Charlie always showed judgment. In things that mattered. He was trapped by the things that do not matter – I wonder would he think that now?

They say I was a triumph when I returned to the stage after his imprisonment. I despised them. They say my public support of him increased my triumph, confirmed my nobility.

Yes, I was a triumph. As for the rest, my pride knew no other course. I learned to despise his enemies, in those times. I learned to be wary of all men, to look behind their idolising faces, to use my triumph for survival.

I have considered others. Now they must consider me.

Poor Charlie, he loved the things in this room and never came within metres of really possessing them. Gobelin tapestry, antique chairs, throne for a Renaissance bishop; they are jests. What I inherit I will absorb whole, then go to the theatre absorbed in the many other selves I may grow capable of. I have not yet achieved one-tenth of the world I am learning. I will not give it up. I will be spendthrift and value the juice and the pith and the rind. Poor Charlie wanted to be loved. Even his own father could not forgive that.

1899. Brisbane, Australia

Sid Prior leans on a split-rail fence near Ma Bain's Pub, Myrtletown

Last night I got full as a state school hatrack, fair belt I got full. Woke up, bolt upright, 5 a.m. and straight into that fencing job. Mouth like an Afghan's armpit. It's the arsenic old Ma Bain shoves in her beer – 'to preserve it'. Preserves the beer, destroys the drinker. No wonder I drink shandygaffs. Got to break it down with rum or gin or whatever. Got to get it through the hurdle. Well, it's only a loan.

That cove there – that's the one, down at the wharf. You think he's one of Dr Bancroft's mates? Hey Wenzel, that your new Pastor? Look at him but. I tell y', all sorts ends up here, down with the mangroves and the she-oaks and the Chinese prawners and us lot. You say, Wenzel?

Nah, and how's them grapes of yours, the black buggers – what is it – Hamburgs? Tell yuz, that land of yours is mostly salt. So barren the wallabies'd need a cut lunch there, tell yuz.

G'day.

I said, G'day there.

He deaf or somethink? Sprechen zu deutsch?

What's that you say, Wenzel? Bob Bain, ten minutes flat he'll have the news out of that one. He *must* be one of Dr Bancroft's lot. Them clothes. Must be. Snotty as a cockatoo staring down a beer bottle. Go on, Wenzel, you front up and ask him; go on.

Well, and so?

No one comes down here for a holiday. This is the end, end of the world. If you'll excuse the expression gentlemen, the arsehole of the universe, the quoit, the rectum. Y'come down here to die. Or in your case, Wenzel, to try Hamburg grapes in salty bog. In mine, to split timber and to drink meself to death.

There he goes, straight as a pound of candles. He won't get far that way. Mozzies. He'll be back. Walks in a walking daze, that one, bet he doesn't know whether it's Christmas or George Street. What did he say to ya, Wenzel?

Selling you Life? Don't believe it! Not much life down where he's heading but.

That's it. I'm first in the queue for the next shandygaff.

Part I: Family

'We may not fit the vision, but there's no way back.'

PULSZKY Károly: London 1853–Brisbane, Australia 1899. Art historian, writer, member of the Hungarian Academy of Sciences 1883, the son of Ferenc Pulszky. Diploma of Arts and Sciences, Leipzig. Until 1881 was Curator of the Museum of Applied Arts, then became first Director of the National Gallery. With his excellent skill he acquired many very important art works (Piombo: *Portrait of a Man*) and made his collection well known with his scientific critique. Between 1881–4 he edited the *Archaeological Review*. He migrated to Australia because of political persecution. He was the first husband of Emilia Markus.

MARKUS Emilia: Szombathely 1860–Budapest 1949. The most celebrated (with Mari Jaszai) actress of the National Theatre. In 1882 she married Károly Pulszky who was Director of the National Gallery, and after his death she married Oszkár Párdány. She had a large repertory and was equally successful in each of her rôles. Her beauty and wonderful hair led to her being called 'the blonde beauty'. She had a rôle in the first Hungarian film, *The Dance*, in 1901.

PULSZKY Ferenc: 1814–1897. Throughout his life he was active in public affairs: President of the reorganised Association of Applied Art; Vice President of the Archaeological and Historical Association. He founded the Museum of Applied Arts. Member of the Academy of Sciences. In 1869 he was appointed Director of the National Museum (retired 1894). Much travelled, including a period in exile after the 1849 Kossuth uprising where he became active in London and America in promoting the Hungarian nationalist cause. On his return to Budapest his salon became the heart of the cultural circles of the city. His many writings are excellent not only stylistically but from the point of view of his determined judgment and political views which were liberal and antisectarian.

(from *Nagy Lexikon*)

Marius Jokai on the rise of the city of Budapest

'Even in the year 1848 a great Hungarian statesman said, "Budapest is not Hungary in the way that Paris is France." Yet, since then, things have progressed to such an extent that today everyone says, "Budapest is the heart of Hungary" . . .

'Thirty years ago the city of Pest was still shrouded in the dust-clouds of a sandy desert, the Rákos; today this sand has been stabilized by streets and trees. And in the Buda mountains, where previously there was hardly any life, the rack-railway runs past rows of magnificent country houses, and an excellent water system sprays streams of water over fresh gardens. Thirty years ago all that seemed just a dream. The stranger seeing Budapest for the first time is astounded at the beautiful situation of this twin city. There on a proud height rises the royal palace of Buda, the Blocksberg looks out over the limitless plain of the Alföld, between two rows of palaces the mighty Danube surges beneath three solid bridges, the middle one of which is the suspension bridge, a masterpiece of bridge-building, and in the midst of the river sleeps the romantic Margaret Island while a swarm of steamboats bustle about. Smoking chimneys announce far and wide that the capital has a well-developed manufacturing industry, and the teeming throngs of workers on the river embankments indicate a booming trade. The view of Budapest in the evening from the suspension bridge is especially magical, when the twin rows of lamps along both banks mingle in the distance with the lights of the other bridges and call forth in the dark mirror of the Danube the redoubled illusion of a seaside bay. The most picturesque panorama, though, is to be seen from the eastern slopes of the Schwabenberg: at the foot of the mountain, divided by the blue Danube, lies the twin city with its high-domed Cathedral, its belt of green woods, and the varied outline of the Buda mountains.

'In thirty years Budapest has become a rich city and a Hungarian city. Both assertions may be powerfully reinforced by quoting some figures. The Hungarian capital has spent during this time nearly 30 million florins on the chief source of national culture, its schools. And while the city has been developing its national character it has also striven to keep in step with European culture.'

(quoted by Kurt Blaukopf in *Mahler: a Documentary Study*)

The musician Victor von Herzfeld of the Budapest Music Academy writes up his diary

The week progresses better than I dared hope. The Master is in good humour again tonight. I now find his gruffness somewhat endearing, bear-like not formidable. This afternoon Kössler and I put our heads together and determined to lure him to the Mahler *Don Giovanni* at the Opera House. Brahms had been quite resolute in his opposition to the plan. 'I do not need to watch the thing mimicked on a stage, the score itself and my own inner ear and eye give me a perfect realisation', the Master said, and then went on with some slighting remarks about 'the little Jew'. One forgives such things in a set old man.

But we were determined. The Mahler production has all Budapest and half of musical Europe by the ears. The perfect integration of singing style, acting style, production details. The man's a genius; I could go to his theatre every night and still walk out dazed and excited, the wonderment showing clearly on my face, as I'm sure each one of my students sees and no doubt parodies – except that they, themselves, are similarly struck.

Well, Brahms this evening was lured out of his rooms and their reek of cigar and coffee dregs, by the promise of a night at the beer tavern. He agreed to that, soon enough.

But we made sure to lead him past the Opera House, it being 7 p.m. and the work set to begin.

'Probably we are too early for the beer to be settled, the tap will gush foam if we are too soon in', I said, affecting casualness. 'Come in for just a half hour to hear the Mahler version.' Well,

25

the Master grumbled a bit, but 'All right, then', he consented, 'so long as there is a sofa at the back of the box. I'll take a nap.'

But after the overture, the strangest grunting sound behind. And then there he was, up beside us, grunting indeed with pleasure and approval, tapping his knee and finally almost in paroxysms of admiration.

'Excellent, quite excellent, tremendous – this Mahler's the very deuce of a fellow!' That was a stunning confession on the Master's part; I've never heard Brahms so ecstatic. He leapt from his place when the act was finished and we all hurried backstage. He embraced Mahler, almost cuffed the frail little man to the floor with his prodigious admiration. 'The finest Don Giovanni of my life!' he kept repeating, and vowed to tell all Vienna, all Europe of his personal discovery, this Gustav Mahler, who had entered the very soul of Mozart's score and done the impossible: convince Brahms it was possible indeed to make the performance equal his inner vision.

Lilli Lehmann, who was Donna Anna, came up then. As she remarked to me later, the genuinely amazing thing about Mahler's production, which he supervises stringently down to the last member of the chorus, is that his policy of insisting on Hungarian as the sung language means, in fact, all visiting celebrities like herself who sing Italian or German, should increase the incoherence of the work but the reverse applies. It is his art to discern patterns and balance in movement, gesture, costume, even lighting, to match the musical thought.

Later, elated, we forgot the beer hall entirely and went in a grand party to the salon of the Pulszkys, who had a neighbouring box. Emilia Markus, whom I have only admired on the stage, is indeed a bravura performer in all contexts – she handled Brahms with consummate tact – and of course her husband Károly is well known throughout Budapest, always dashing here and there full of plans and busyness: he seemed more reserved tonight, and I think Brahms may have bluffed him with his gruff exterior, but their apartment is sumptuous and exotic, almost crazy with its palms and tapestries and clutter, but I think Brahms was amused – he said later it had an ingenuous appeal, not like a museum but a warehouse shed. I was stunned at that, and showed it. I could not imagine Pulszky or the Markus in a shed of any kind, though I suppose I am again deceived by the exquisite: after all,

26

Pulszky must spend much of his time in musty warehouses and storage rooms of the Museum. Somehow, by the end, Mahler and his *Don Giovanni* were crowded out by the animation and excitement of the Pulszky group. It was only later, as we walked back through a crisp snowfall, that it came flooding back, and Brahms kept repeating his admiration and delight ...

1894. Budapest

Károly Pulszky on energy

It is a process of discovering that which directs the operable self. I have been accused of driving myself too hard, too far. I have been called an electric light, something burning with energy and yet constant and unconsumed. There are those who accuse me of being restless, of neglecting repose, because by contrast they are unable to keep to my pace. I do not criticise them. I am in no competition, at least not with others. I have my own goals, and they are still beyond the greatest outreach of my abilities or my energies. A man must have impossible goals to learn what is possible.

I have learned to pare down my thrust so that there is no moment wasted, no dross, no slackness allowed. It is a matter of living fully. There is the matter of energy, also. I long ago realised we are part of some greater magnetic field, the individual 'I' being only the visible form of greater connections that push and tug in the dance of life pulses, and these link us beyond place and time into eternal patternings.

I mean, that the magnet channels us. To learn this is to learn how to remove from 'self' and into greater powers; then to express those powers as part of our finite living. I do not claim to be god, only the link with God we all share.

In learning this I have been enabled to concentrate those energies, almost to absent myself from myself in order that the energies might flow with and from that magnet power.

This sounds too abstract? Let me explain it another way.

You have noticed what you call my drive, my capacity to keep working, to keep thinking, to keep exploring my craft with almost incessant zeal. My reading power has become prodigious, and I remember everything. I do not say this as a boast, indeed, it is with quite pure humility. I am a vessel. I have, only, learned to make use of the divine magnet, the energy source that carries through us all, and to allow it a white focus, you could almost say a white hot concentration, light if you can imagine it pushed into absolute focus like the sun through a magnifying glass, but even tighter: a power so intense it can ignite.

Burn myself out? Not at all. What I speak of is the focus that allows such energy its full power, and I have discovered this to be a power to refine, not to destroy.

I am an instrument.

One way, as an example, to show you what I have learned. Sleep. You think it important that the body should have rest and sleep, that otherwise it falls apart, the parts do not function, the eyes tire, the limbs lose coordination, the mind becomes sluggish and then dull and then later clogs into inertia. We have all been told these country proverbs. They are untrue. I have honed back my sleep until I can go nights, weeks, months at a time without closing my eyes longer than a few seconds. The body is a storehouse we hardly enter, it holds magnetic powers greater than most of us dare think of. Without sleep I have been able to concentrate my focus in a hundred new directions. My alertness, my intelligence is not impaired. Rather, it is wakened, as if from a torpid doze, some midsummer somnolence that drugs the senses, rather than refreshes them. I burn like electric light, and as powerfully. And this is just a beginning.

The Eastern mystics knew these things. To fast and stay wakeful is the way to approach God. In the Spice Islands – Java – the power of the *dukun*, the healer, is generated by fasting and by wakefulness, often for many days on end.

Last month I slept no more than a few hours, and that in the smallest snatches. I feel no strain at this, only a sort of energy release. Look into my eyes, you do not see them reddened, glazed, distorted. Look at my writing script: my hand is as neat and small and well formed as ever, copybook italic. And this is the catalogue I have begun in those unsleeping nights, already several hundred pages of close text, a full and comprehensive description of each item in the Museum, with an entirely thorough referencing. It is, if I may say it, a model of its kind. Look. This is the latest sample, which I have just completed. A puzzle I found most intriguing to resolve.

The artist is Jakab Bogdány and his dates are 1660 to 1724. This painting was executed in 1700. That much we know. He was – and this is interesting in itself – the first great Hungarian artist after the Turkish occupation. A master of still-life pictures: flowers, fruit, exotic birds. Well, Bogdány settled in England where he mastered his art and indeed he was able to hold his own with the most distinguished of the Dutch and Flemish genre painters. I was once shown, in Hampton Court, the *Looking-glass Closet* he executed for their Queen Mary in, I think, 1690.

Well, this still-life in our collection is a marvel. I recognised its value instantly. You see how all the birds are poised or directing the eye to the lower centre, that pile of exquisite fruit – translucent grapes, peaches, pears, the figs? A masterpiece of composition. And you note how the great red macaw dominates the left-hand side, balanced by the subtle but strong white of the cockatoo and the green king parrot which perch on the umber-coloured ruins opposite. Well, my research has even gone to elucidating each species of bird depicted. That cockatoo and king parrot. They are Australian. A curious thing, one of the reasons I find this detection work so satisfying: did you know that the official discovery of Australia was seventy years after this work was painted?

How do you explain that? Well, my father tells me that no doubt some passing seaman traded the parrots with a native or islander in those seas, and I am sure he is right. Birds were much prized in London in that time, and the parrot species are a long-lived, robust sort of bird.

Yet this – here – is an even stranger thing: this one, this, by Tóbiás Stranover, who was a pupil of Bogdány in London: here we have again a king parrot and another bird – a kookaburra, which is a species of giant kingfisher. These also are peculiar to Australia, that island-continent. Imagine! They were painted decades before that land was even thought about! Stranover also died in 1724. Disturbing, isn't it? His piece is a mawkish composition, but still a strangely haunting evocation of wilderness landscape, a sort of primal Eden before the fall – though we do notice the snake in the corner, a rather tedious snake. Still, I am haunted by his dreamed-of land; I wonder did he ever hear strange legends or sailors' tales about that unmapped wilderness? We shall never know. Some continents we know before we know them, they are within us as much as we inhabit them. The country of the impossible dream, without laws and without restrictions.

29

The *terra incognita* that might, in a flash, turn to terror incognita: that is what this Stranover hints at.

A clumsy little work, but I have always been haunted. It was my father who helped with the ornithological research.

The other task I have begun, in these exciting and alert hours reclaimed from Morpheus, is a translation of Julian Symonds, *The Renaissance in Italy*. It is a large work, and one I find fascinating. To put it into Hungarian is to re-invent, almost, the excitement of the author's own discoveries. It is as if I, myself, were the creator – just like Stranover – and in a way I am.

1894. Castle Széchény, Hungary

Ferenc Pulszky drafts a letter to his son

Where do I start to lecture him? Poor dear Charlie, he rouses in me an indulgent joy, even when I am most aggrieved. His lack of tact, his boorish inconsideration, his complete failure to understand the loneliness and needs of an old man and why this late marriage has restored me to comforts and small delights that are almost painful in their intensity. His delight with himself and his own plans: good God, I could be furious. But am not, that is the thing.

How to explain? I think it is his lack of deviousness, his impulse to believe in what absorbs him thoroughly. Perhaps, also, there is an element of coquettishness in him, a wish to be patted with approval, a childlike way of trotting to me with his new ideas, his latest plans, like a puppy with a well-mouthed quail or partridge. One is delighted when the dog, by instinct and by breeding, does not damage the kill. I am, frankly, delighted at the skill – and thoroughness – of Charlie's enthusiasms. He is carried away, yes, but the expertness seems ingrained, something born, so that nothing he touches seems to go awry. That first work in the Applied Arts Museum: what might have been a chore to such a lively young fellow he made into a glowing testament of his industry. Indeed, as Eötvös remarked to me, young Charlie in that little Museum created a world of fascination and science where hitherto only a sort of dutiful doggedness seemed possible or likely.

Impossible to be affronted by Charlie. The quality of play and application seem delightfully joined in him. He is one of the charmed young men. And his Emmy has justified exactly his blend of innocence and flair. To marry an actress caused no little fuss – even my daughter was at first horrified. But then to display his most beautiful prize as a woman of unquestionable intellect and liveliness of mind: that was the audacious win. I love the girl. I love her devotedly. Perhaps it's half because of her I first conceived the possibility of a new shared life of my own, an old age blessed with kindness, wit and alertness. Dear Emmy. Emilia.

That, however, is not to say that I am pleased with him. I am furious.

All this dizzying round, well, of course in my widower years I set an example with my Saturday salon. But that was serious. The politics of the country were decided over egri bikaver or some particular tokaji, the battle against anti-Semitism; the secularisation of the schools: my God, battles still not completed and here am I retired now after two decades of the struggle. Sometimes the tiredness returns, the ennui.

It is curious that Charlie fills me both with this sense of exhaustion and with refreshment. The exhaustion, yes, because this last note of his, full of plans and green ambition and such innocence – surely he must know it is mere chance, or political expediency, that his scheme for a National Gallery is approved promptly. He can rest assured that Károly Várády, or Géza Polonyi, in giving support are merely biding time. The enemies of one's life are not always those who oppose your entire principles. They are those who come close to your own ideals, but in the last count look for a knife to thrust in your back, so that they may step into your position and your prestige. The worst ones do not even realise what it is has created your celebrity. They plot, they wrangle, they will certainly draw their knives. And what will they be left with, should they succeed? For themselves, the quench of spite and a terrible need for further victims, enemies, props to set up, else their own spiritual emptiness will be revealed . . . pah, these commonplaces of knowledge!

And here is Charlie still deceived. Will he never learn? Will he never learn caution? temperance? care in his dealings with such men?

That is not his nature. His nature grows from a more intuitive soil. I fear he will be one day seriously injured.

31

I am an old man. I must remind myself that. He is in the pith of his life, he exceeds us all with his flair and risk-taking and his sheer, measurable skill. And his own energy, his brave quickness. The way he challenged Várády to that duel (for the honour of *my* name!) . . . yes, of course I was proud. And angry.

Yet again, trapped by anger and a sort of homage to that young man. I hope he never realises how much he resides in my thoughts, how in a way I have become dependent on his energy and enthusiasm to recharge my own battery sources.

And now I must write, and what will I say?

'My dear son, your bubbling letter fills me with grave concern, you must consider consequences . . .'

1899. June. Brisbane, Australia

Károly Pulszky his own Don Quixote

Don Quixote at the Inn
DOMINICUS VAN WYNEN ('Ascanius') 1661-90
    (Donated by Károly Pulszky to the Hungarian National Gallery)

A picture to make you grin. The Don
will not be put upon. He strikes
his purpose like an ass; no one
denies the fine stand he takes.
Vision shines through his mistakes.

Quixote has purpose to put at naught
the spite of lackeys, women who jeer,
women who mock, women caught
in their dangerous windows, who stare
with dangerous flesh. Devils live there.

Quixote strides grimly but sure
through upside-down land (it's an Inn).
He finds his centre everywhere.
Time is the measure of things, then
action. Through Quixote whole lives spin.

32

That's my world. What mayhem
once you assume the businessman is wrong.
Helmet, and armour, are what you come
with, along the way, and if you bring
only a copping-bowl it's the same thing.

I saw myself the Donor, back
half turned but present, in the event
but not involved. Involved to take
the gesture for the act and half the want
for twice the payment. In the event

I gave my painting away, even in this
aping my father. So much to relish
in the details: the donor surely has
only a feigned indifference, his polish
masking a fear of contact. Is the Don foolish?

Caught in the upside-down land I envy
Quixote his purpose. – There's gusto and there's passion.
I die in this land's lack of purpose, I see
its unreality. Like Quixote I'd be the last to fashion
my own fault. We may not fit the vision

but there's no way back. Not even denial
is an alternative. Caught thus
you are caught full-centre, you've mounted the saddle.
I gave that painting to my city, Budapest,
that others might grin, and become possessed.

1899. Early June. Budapest

Emilia Markus advises her elder daughter, Tessa, who is writing to her father, known to be in Australia

When you write to your father in Australia, dear Tessa, it would be cruel to quote that: 'I was not going away to ease and self indulgence ... I was going away to hardship. I expect no joy: it

33

is gone from my life.' What is it from? Ah! George Eliot. His favourite, *Romola*. No; I see you meant well. But here, give the book to me. You see how the passage continues, the terrible perception of Savonarola?

'You are seeking your own will ... You are seeking some good other than the law you are bound to obey. But how will you find good? It is not a thing of choice ... I say again, man cannot choose his duties. You may choose to forsake your duties, and choose not to have the sorrow they bring. But you will go forth; and what will you find ...? Sorrow without duty – bitter herbs, and no bread with them.'

You must think. Little more than a month, and mail brings messages from the bottom of the world. He is no further away than a postage stamp and a little patience. Our thoughts go forth so much more speedily now than in old times. We must think of the future.

Ours is an age of miracles. The telegraph; the Orient Express; the new Métro system. Truly, in my lifetime the outstanding thrust of man has been towards communication. Did I tell you I have friends who asked me to perform for their cinematograph, a system of photography that records movement as well as space? In your time you will inherit such achievements as if they were everyday. Your father might yet send from across the world such a moving record and it would be as if he were present still.

Why did you choose that text? You had some purpose? Do not turn away. You must love him deeply, do you hear. Now, erase it.

The concept of 'good' is something your father was much given to discussing, did he ever read this passage out to you? It was a book he valued. Its Renaissance setting, its accurate detail. He valued accuracy as well as goodness, as you are aware. His quality of goodness was as abstract as the ideas of his Savonarola. Very well, as George Eliot's Savonarola. 'Goodness' for him had nothing to do with pence or the opinions of others. 'Goodness' is a principle. It is like vision, as inexorable. For him, I think, it meant an equivalent of 'energy', or 'ambition'.

So many things, now, you must do with him in mind. He loved you deeply.

34

It will be a long time.

You must not let Romola forget. Take her to the Gallery. No, I shall not come. You understand I have reasons. Show her especially all the things your father added to that Gallery. He transformed it. Do you know the Piombo, *Portrait of a Man*? Of course you know it, your father took you especially to see it when it arrived. He was very excited. For just a few days he was elated, that time. Do you know why? Surely Charlie told you? No? That portrait is over three hundred years old, and yet it almost seems the very likeness of your father. It is most strange. From the instant I saw it I thought it more than strange. Your father was astounded that I saw the likeness before he even spelled it out to me. But it was so immediate – and it explained so many things. Well, you take another look. The eyes, the nose, chin – even more, the expression. I saw him gaze out like that often, some text in hand. He was not always chatting or telling jokes or dazzling the salon. He was like one of those new electric lights, burning constantly.

You remember only the last few years. In the end it was as if a glass barrier were built around him. I think that is true, and we must not deny it. It was a sort of isolation, perhaps a preparation for his new and solitary task in life. For your father, as with his heroine Romola in the novel, all joy did fade. You must write to him, often.

His fate is not choice. Remember that. But it is a sort of destiny, something set to be endured, sustained, overcome. I am sure your father is aware of these things and is setting his mind to them.

'Sorrow without duty – bitter herbs, and no bread with them . . .' They are strange lines, excellent as they are, and poetic. I wonder what herbs flourish in that country, Australia? How many choices of bread? Your father had it in him to be frugal, simple, with the rich simplicity of a Magyar peasant, those who endure.

Light, but without fire.

The habit of luxury engulfed us readily enough. We were like children. My father-in-law called us 'candle flames; innocents'. You smile.

Well now, where are you up to. Do you have much news to write him? Have you mentioned my new performances? That will give him comfort. Tell him my voice is bearing up wonderfully now, and that the audiences are so ecstatic it challenges me to higher achievements. No, don't tell him that. Say I miss his applause in the wings. Say my engagement has been extended this season, and that means his debts begin to be less burdensome; in a year or two we may be clear. And send him my love.

1899. June 4th. Brisbane, Australia
Károly Pulszky thinks of his father

Sometimes I do ask myself, what if my father were still alive, would my pitiful history have been altered? Or would he have disavowed me?

That is impossible.

Yet I think of his own volume of autobiography, and the way the family refused ever to speak of his older brother, after he committed suicide. One pistol shot snapped shut the door to my uncle's life, and all traces were removed, it was as if he had never been.

Sometimes I long for a silence like that.

I am frightened of that.

My father, surely, would have supported me. The case against me was almost a repetition of his own in the '80s, with the Csontosi business, when Várády and Polonyi first set themselves openly to smear the Pulszky name. We all knew that Janos Csontosi was merely a puppet, an employee of the Museum and a family friend: they sought my father's downfall with their sordid charges of gross negligence, made under parliamentary privilege. I was full of pith and fibre then. It seems curious to think I challenged Várády to that duel on Margaret Island – something that never occurred to me when my own honour was implicated by that same man. Perhaps I was always secretly defensive, vulnerable. My father withstood the buffetings of parliamentary enemies like a massive giant, as if the barbs did not hit him at all, yet I knew they did. And I knew in some ways the charges against him were indeed cunning; there was a dangerous perfunctoriness in his Directorship of the National Museum. But he held his own power and position. He had earned that from a lifetime of enterprise. He was not flung off by small darts.

Again and again I ask myself: why with me did they strike home?

My father was an old warrior. His one objective: you win. I remember him talking to others (I was in the room) of the Baroness von Beck, in his London exile. 1850s, years of my birth and that of my brother. From the beginning we were conscious of exile and an impending destiny, always triumphant. The Baroness von Beck's *Hungarian Diary* became the talk of London, it eclipsed my mother's own volume that had been compared with Madame de Staël. My father was one who finally declared this Baroness a fraud. He had been forewarned that a German edition of her *Personal Adventures in the Late Hungarian War* contained an attack on him. His counter-attack was decisive. She was brought to court to be exposed. But much damage was done, and the fact that this phony 'Baroness' took a heart attack in the witness-box and died, was justice of a kind. It provoked, however, sympathy for her case, and much rancour, but my father said to me, once, a man in public life must grow like an armadillo or a hedgehog.

I thought of my own work as a private destiny. My public life was the cultural interchange of Budapest and the world. My father always spoke to me as to a small, enthusiastic boy. Even in entertaining I emulated him. He gave such witty, busy parties. So many things I tried to please him with.

I was industrious. He conceded that. What was I asking of him? When he died, I knew the loss was great, but I did not understand what loss entailed. I thought I harboured some secret anger towards my father (especially when he remarried; that lugubrious mismatch). It was not anger at all. It was something to mould myself upon and grow towards, though I was a person entirely different.

In his late years he was a heavy old man.

Now, if I think of him, it is his voice repeating that famous early speech of Kossuth (which I believe my father half-wrote). The words always thrilled me. Now I understand the words. 'The Hungarian people has two duties to fulfil. The first, to rise to crush invaders; the second, to remember!' Strange, that I never sensed this second command might be the most cruel. Nor that its consequences could be more than a compelling rhetoric:

37

'Should you neglect these things, your name will be synonymous with shame and wickedness ... so base, that even your Maker shall repent of having created you, so accursed that air shall refuse your strength, that the cornfield under your hand shall turn to desert, that the refreshing wellhead shall dry at your approach!

'Then shall you wander homeless about the world, imploring compassion in vain, and dry bread. The race of strangers then will smite you on the face.'

Words always come back to smite you. I think of the words I translated in *Romola*. They are the same. 'You will go forth, and what will you find ...? ... bitter herbs, and no bread with them.'

Sometimes I ask myself, how would my father find me, now? I pick up the *Brisbane Courier* and it announces with a hint of mockery the death of the Waltz King, Johann Strauss.

1899. Brisbane, Australia

Károly Pulszky remembers the carbuncle gem

In one of my mother's stories
a great gem was lost.
On the impossible mountain
it glowed in the sun. The hunter
consumed himself in its fire,
sold his soul, shot to dislodge it.
His sure bullet sent the jewel
into the bottomless lake.
I recall how I ached with that legend.
My mother died before I turned fourteen.
I still called for her stories.
They transfigured me.

Narcissus looked into the lake's dark waters
not for reflections of his own self-knowledge
but for echoes of that lost, deeper light.

38

Sometimes in this underworld of clear light
and inconsolable ache I know I have plunged
through that lake. It is not bottomless.
It is a shadeless park and a sky mocking me.
It is my own world inverted and without consolation.
In my pocket the carbuncle gem has become
a snake jewelled trinket that I rub
for what it reminds me of – fire
in the impossible mountains, desire
and greed that goes on forever.
My mother's story never passed on
to the later events – the long flight
of the accursed hunter. Some parts
you are required to finish yourself.

In the legend of Actaeon, the hunter
becomes the stag and is torn open.
Actaeon looked on the goddess and was damned.
I drown in the bottomless lake of the story
and discover it is the voice
of something long ago forgotten –
the telling voice of that clever jewel
my mother.

> Miss Romola Pulszky
> c/- Mme Emilia Markus
> Royal Hotel
> Budapest V
> HUNGARY

Brisbane, 4th June, 1899

My sweet little Romola!

Mother told me in her last letter that you have been studying seriously again this year, and diligently, and you will pass your exams successfully. I am very proud that my little girl so completely fulfils my expectations of her.

39

Believe me, you might be brainy, but thoroughness and a persistent effort are more important in obtaining results and to become the true joy of your relatives.

Being such a clever little girl I know you will always make an effort to make your mother happy. I hope that you are still able – just as you used to when I was still at home – to comfort your mother when something troubles her.

Do this always, as you and Tessa can do this best. Don't ever envy Tessa for her mother's love for her, but love them both, as you'll never have better friends in this world.

I am far away from you my poor little one, so much so that I don't know if I'll ever see you again. But don't ever forget that I love you very much, and I am proud that you are always kind and good.

God bless you,
many kisses from
Charlie

Romola Nijinsky-Pulszky receives a wallet containing photographs that had belonged to her father

To suicide in Australia is to invoke great ghosts in children. Well, small children survive. They must stretch outwards. My father was not thinking of me or of ghosts when he shot himself. He was forty-five. At forty-five I discovered my husband's diary and published it.

'God is in me. I have made mistakes but I corrected them with my life . . . It is all the same to me where I live, I live where God wishes. I will travel all my life if God wishes . . .'

Vaslav signed it, 'God and Nijinsky'.

Our eldest daughter, Kyra, was newly married; her father in his terrible illness was more remote than my father ever was. I

40

can afford, now, to shed tears for that poor grave on a stony hill with no shade.

Always such restless travel. All of us.

'The little horse is tired,' said Vaslav. The little horse had been cruelly birched. But some of us cannot be released like that.

> *I was not born in this place.*
> *I have migrated here from another country*
> *and that is how one fares in a strange country:*
> *he has no sweetheart would cling to his arms.*

Why do I think of that? All our folksongs prepare us for exile, nothing prepares us for loss. Two months my father lived in that country, Australia. I was still a small, wrinkled creature, they said I had fragile health. Did I cause him ache? Did he think of me at all, was I anything to him, then?

> *Where shall I die?*
> *If I die in the woods, beasts will devour me*
> *and the birds of the sky will lament for me.*

All I really remember of my father is that he told me stories out of Vasari – Fra Filippo Lippi taken captive to Barbary, who then astonished his new master by drawing him with raw charcoal on a wall, when neither drawing nor painting were yet known in those barbarous parts. Yes, Lippi was then set free. My father liked triumphal, moral stories.

Those barbarous parts. I think too much on that poor, unhappy man. I did not know him. He had no conception of me.

'I want to give my wife a house complete with everything, she is afraid I will soon die. She thinks I am mad. She has this idea because she thinks too much. I think little, and therefore understand everything I feel. I am the flesh. I am the feeling. I am God in flesh and feeling.'

There are walls, Vaslav, walled prisons and unwalled ones. Even I have been confined, if never willingly. My father spoke to me of walled gardens, a fountain, the strange white deer of Magor. We both believed it (secretly) a Unicorn. I married. If I wanted anything I knew how to get it, even if I forged the key or broke the lock. My mother was the most famous actress in Hungary, but my husband danced for the world. I devoted my whole life to him.

41

I could never forgive my mother's secret betrayal of my father. There are some things I cannot imagine.

> *They have bound my wreath*
> *its twigs bend round my shoulder;*
> *they have bound green rosemary in it*
> *and put a bunch of sorrows in the centre.*

Vaslav leaping in chains. Vaslav bound into his chains. My father chained.

It takes a lifetime to learn quietness. My mother was still an actress at eighty. She abandoned the stage only when she began to forget her lines. 'You see, you see, it begins to get dark', she said then and they wept, the other actors, the stage manager, the producer wept bitterly and could not find the words she had forgotten, though they read the script to her.

I did not go to my mother's funeral.

My husband had been greater, but his chains were greater. His dark began so much earlier; and no one listened.

This wallet that was my father's, why should I grow sentimental over it? I cannot control my tears, it is my childhood in old leather, it is his last instructions to me and their sternness, their authority. He was the saint in the forest glow, my St Eustace, and the deer was a vision. I must believe that, just as I must believe in the ferocity of Vaslav, in the spark that once glowed, in its time and in its way. Such a short time, but so entirely. There was a different power in my mother, a power that was my own. I never held her stage, though I created platforms in poor Vaslav's name. I never shared anything with my father.

Poor Charlie.

Old leather, and the craftsman's name still embossed: 'Alois Merton by appointment to the King & Emperor'. Even the dead plunge us into ironies, and I have no dinner guests to entertain who would acknowledge irony sufficiently.

How can I say, 'I remember Alois Merton, his shop?'

Baba. An inscription, here, inside, and I know instantly that was not my mother's phrase, she never used such a term. Baba: baby. Well, perhaps it had been a gift, then, this wallet, a secret other. I could never have imagined. They were inseparable. They were electric – as a child the electricity frightened me, it seemed so full of themselves without me.

He must have been always a stranger.

Well, I can imagine that, too, why not? When I set my mind on something, nothing and nobody matters. I thought too much. How can I disguise my joy to discover this old photo of myself in my father's wallet? Indeed that is the real joy of fondling it, though it is a print familiar to me from albums. With Tessa and (of course) our mother. Seventy years. Why should not my father have been a great man in Budapest? I know that was a true statement of his achievement.

Nothing. Nobody.

It is his voice rubbed into leather and it is not addressing me. Yet I swear I still hear it, his true voice. It is so many other voices.

> *Get up father, get up mother,*
> *the Ancient Ones have come.*
> *They are the Old Law,*
> *they hide in songs.*

> *Stork, stork, turtle-dove*
> *why are your feet bleeding?*
> *Turkish children cut them,*
> *Magyar children heal them*
> *with pipes, drums and reed violins . . .*

1899. June 10th

Supposed case of suicide
A magisterial inquiry

'An Inquiry was held on Saturday, at the Central Police Court, Brisbane, by Mr J. Sidle, J.P., into the death of a man named Charles Poulszky, who was found lying dead near the highway at Myrtletown on the 6th instant, with a loaded revolver in his hand and a bullet wound in the heart. The deceased belonged to a prominent Hungarian family ... Dr Hirschfeld spoke of having identified the body in company with the German Consul at the hospital. Deceased was employed as a canvasser, but had only been two months in the colony. He was about 45 years of age, and son of an officer in the Austrian Army, though he was born in London. The man had been married, and there were two children, one about 15 and the other about 8 years old. The inquiry then closed.'

(from the Brisbane *Courier*)

James Proud on oath saith: I am a Police Constable stationed in Brisbane. On Tuesday evening last the 6th instant I went to the Hospital Morgue, where I saw the dead body of a man. I was afterwards told the name of deceased was Charles Pulszky. I made a search of the body. I found a revolver which I now produce, one chamber of which had been discharged, the others being loaded. I also found a Chamois revolver case and cartridges, a pair of kid gloves, a tobacco pouch and pocketbook, a Watch (metal), a pair of eyeglasses. A snake jewelled armlet. A pair of sleeve links and sixpence in silver. Two boxes of matches and cigarette paper, a linen handkerchief.

James Proud

Taken on oath and signed before me at Police Court, Brisbane this 10th day of June, A.D. 1899

James Sedlay, J.P.

Part II:
Károly Pulszky in Brisbane 1899

'Time is the measure of things,
then action.'

'... Mr Pulszky and the rest of our party continued their route to New Orleans. When I woke in the morning, everything appeared to me unusually quiet. I first fancied it must be a holiday; the open shops, however, told me I was mistaken; but the busy movement of the commercial places in the North, was not visible here; all seemed still, lifeless, and idle.

'... We strolled about the place; it was burningly hot, so we kept to the lanes, where the groves of myrtle and the edges of roses in full bloom shadowed our way. – We felt transplanted as by a charm into the sunny South. A week back we had left St Louis cold and wintry, now all around us was bloom, luxuriant vegetation and magnificent growth. The houses are charming; galleries on columns run around the high wooden structures, standing in midst of gardens, where the exuberant splendour of Southern nature supplies the lack of art. We found the climate too oppressive to continue our walk ...'

'... whilst in the Old World all physical labour is considered ungentlemanlike, in America, on the contrary, not to work is looked upon as thoroughly degrading. An idle man never can meet there with sympathy, whatever his previous position may have been; and if a man cannot work with his brains, he is expected to labour with his hands. In a country where every one who will work, can earn his livelihood, age, sickness, or vice, alone can lead to helplessness.'
(from *White, Red, Black: Sketches of Society in the United States during the Visit of their Guest*, Francis and Theresa Pulszky)

Dr Eugen Hirschfeld in consultation with Károly Pulszky

— Well, be seated. No, in this chair – I prefer to observe patients in good light. This climate has an excellent sunlight for purging disorders; if you observe its disciplines. Do you sweat?

— If you'll forgive me, I . . .

— I said, man, do you sweat? Sweat, sir? Do you perspire – you do speak English?

— Dr Hirschfeld, my language is not the point. I will converse in Latin or Greek if you prefer. But your name was given me by a London friend . . .

— Aha! This is a social visit. Really you should have notified me in advance, left your card. My daytime hours are devoted to medicine. At night my house is open to more sociable intercourse.

— I am sorry, sir. Your time . . .

— Do not keep apologising, it is a habit that disgusts me. Life is too brief for that. You look sickly. Here, do not move. Let me have a closer examination . . .

— My body is nothing.

— Don't be a fool! Your body is the axle-wheel to your entire health. And in this climate you will disregard it at your peril. This is a climate for the Gods. But the Gods, remember, were no soft pampered darlings. Perhaps the meaning of 'god' is 'one who is perfect in health'. That, I assure you, is where our vision starts, and where it ends too.

— It is not my body . . .

— Traps. It is indeed your body, and you must master it. The body is a balance, a set of scales. Your eyes, for instance – how much do you drink? What have you eaten today, and yesterday? Now: be specific.

— Dr Hirschfeld, you amuse me. The Colonies produce blunt young men.

— Bluntness cuts through convention. But it is imprecise. I am no Scottish boor, no English farmer. Sharpness is more my line, a pair of fine secateurs my ideal. Which is what my old friend Robert Louis Stevenson once told me, so I can quote it as a text ...

— Yes, Stevenson. My London friend had told me you were well connected with anyone of interest ...

— Everyone has interest. That is my opening premise. Every-one. Why else succumb to Medicine as a career? I have a relative in Vienna whose entire study is sexual aberration – well, my interest has limits. But I still begin from a common base: health. Now, sir, my questions – drink? diet?

— Do you know, you've made me smile, and I can tell you that's no small feat. Very well, I will consent to your examination, though to be frank my own health has always been something to which I remain indifferent. Drink – once to excess. These last five years: almost nothing. A little weak tea. Mineral water.

— 'A glass of wine for thy stomach's sake.' Two glasses for the head. Three glasses for denial of both. So you have faced your own lack of discipline? Undiscipline's common enough here. Excess, I'm afraid, is the norm. In the Garden of Eden the fruit of the apple was not knowledge, but denial of it. Hence, man's propensity to excess. It is a running from knowledge. The taste was, it seems, too much for our frailty.

— I have, in twenty-four hours, eaten nothing. Appetite is a burden.

— Complete abstinence is another excess. What is your age?

— I think I am eighty. I discover myself a child. The records state: forty-five.

— Do you lack energy? No, do not answer. I recommend one glass of wine with your meal, and at least one meal each day. In this climate I recommend at evening. To feast at midday is to blot up all energy for hours. I see by your clothes – your gloves, those shoes, cuff links – that your air diet is not penury but choice. An extravagant choice. Perhaps not entirely honest either?

— I assure you, food revolts in my stomach ...

— A little bread, some small crusty bun, or a slice of fresh Vienna ...

— No, don't be a Mephisto – and of course you do catch me out. Last night, it is true, I walked for some hours in the area of

49

Petrie Bight and Wickham Terrace – close by here – I had some crust and a wrapped slice of cheese . . . they were not on me, somehow, on my return. I must have . . .

– So.

– And in the forenoon, a Chinese greengrocer . . .

– Enough. Perhaps it is what you believe of yourself that we should study.

– I do not wish to speak of myself. I had been told you were a sociable man, Dr Hirschfeld, and that I might perhaps find in company and debate a way to forget myself and my burdens . . .

– There is one way to ease personal burdens, sir, and that is to unburden them on others. You are welcome to call on me socially, perhaps even a meal. Your looks – and manner – tell an intriguing story already. I would be honoured if you would unburden your story . . .

– No.

– I promise you, in my practice . . .

– No, my whole life is a burden on others.

– That may be. I am not to judge, nor do I want to. My suggestion to unburden yourself is not made out of a wish to pry. Come, sir, do not mock me, I have the homesickness of every German in Brisbane and West Moreton to put up with. In my fifteen years here – ten of them in Brisbane – I have gauged pretty accurately the gradations of estrangement and exile, the point at which a positive spirit emerges. You are fresh here, yes?

– I am stale here beyond measure. I am an exile, from Budapest.

– Ah, I have a cousin . . .

– My wife and two daughters still live there. I cannot return.

– I can ask why?

– . . .

– You do not have to explain. Even if you are innocent, unjustly forced into exile, your whole comportment bespeaks disgrace. But, curiously, also resentment, a sense of unwarranted injury. Disgrace, but not justice. Shame, but not guilt. You see, I am predisposed to believe your claims, whatever they are. I believe in the science of bodies. You remember, that was our point of introduction.

Pulszky on Vasari

'Nothing so inspires men or makes the burden of their studies seem lighter, than the prospect that their work will eventually bring respect and riches.'

Vasari wrote that, and I noted it for my two daughters. A firm observation, and a true one.

'Men cultivate their talents with redoubled ambition when they are spurred on by applause.'

My energy was more than I imagined. For the first time I not only understood, I felt with Vasari, that last Italian visit. Like the refining intensity of a vortex my energy increased, it dragged in others, certainly it hurtled me (I was constantly surprised at the passion) into my great project. And wherever I went, prizes. I hardly believed my own fortune, or the fortune of Hungary that would spend centuries savouring the wealth I discovered, bargained for, appropriated, in its name. Millennium year would give Hungary its great Gallery, and the voice in it would be my own.

In Italy I grasped for the first time the power of my choice over generations of future students and acolytes. More than any individual artist it was my power of selection that would achieve the memorable view. Italy was my first conquest, my casquet. The last triumph – my great stroke – was the portrait by Piombo. Some claimed it a Rafael, that was not the point: it was a masterwork and the price (if I dealt skilfully) made me spin with astonishment. The Comtesse de Chevigné partnered me, one might even say played into my hands in this, but I knew my invincibility. I was drunk in that moment with the sure knowledge of what I was doing. Others would drink, also, at the fountain of my insight. I was suffused with this sense of vision.

'Talent, all the same, only too often provokes envy . . . men who have talent must either prove complete superiority or, at least, demonstrate that their achievements are soundly based and will stand up to criticism.'

51

I have some pride. But I could not contend with purse-strings, blotting-paper, a Parliament of barleyhusks and soft pewter. I did not believe the Parliament's rejection of my whole enterprise because of a receipt and a budget year and the small change of some accounting parsimony. O brave millennium year! They knifed me with goosequills. They lost decades of my vision.

It was my father they intended. At least I have acted, in this, as his shield-guard, deflecting their more malicious intent. The last two years of his life spilled into their files but they must have known he would be indomitable. I could not bear to face him, in the end. It was me they sought out, it was my own purpose torn to shreds, why need my father accuse me for that? Betrayal, when it comes, surprises in ways Vasari could not prepare me for. He was, after all, himself a dauber of execrable frescoes.

Károly Pulszky in early June, Australian winter

A morning of varnished light, each hill reveals its purpose like a landscape by Giorgione. The town is clearly important to each roof-chimney; after the manner of Carpaccio. Each tree is by Bellini, the road with its blond cuttings is precise as Mantegna. We see by associations. I once loved Italy.

But, having seen, we inhabit a land. I could become lost here truly, taking this into me, transmuting the mornings of ocean-drenched light. The sun shakes its salty limbs out of the world's largest ocean. The ocean itself calls through white teeth like naked boys on the Lido, as carefree. I could become these hills that only an artist might unveil to his fellows. No photograph will ever uncover the stillness of mornings like this, the *feel* of air with its sea wash, the blue and gold I am drenched in. This is a miraculous country.

On my face, fingers of godlike air, a perfume clean as the lines of Piero.

Those born here must find their own names: how many generations before the names for this morning are discovered? Its richness lifts me up, I am the visionary who might have authority, by this canvas of air, to hold it forever. It is not mine.

I possess it no more than these surly colonial Britishers, who dream rain-misted villages into this landscape and must be dismayed. This is a place should be seen through the eyes of an artist from Tuscany, Umbria, the Veneto. The long plains of Hungary breed eyes to see clearly such distances. I could dream the wild deer of Magor into the foothills and sea plains of Brisbane.

Things I bring with me.

I once had made, by the finest miniaturist in Budapest, a gentle parody of Melozzo de Forli; with myself as Donor, Emmy as the Muse, the Madonna. Melozzo modelled, himself, after Rafael. My miniaturist's name: *Innocent*. In Hungary, that means nothing.

This morning I will walk into these hills. I will be humble. I will regain some innocence. These hills must teach me themselves. I must savour their otherness, each tree has its own lore.

Who are the others I would instruct? Who listens to me? On a morning of Apollo light I must discard my seven languages – I must discard Apollo. Even naked, the limbs I imagine are those of some boy on the hot summer banks of the Duna – Donau – Danube – It is a canvas by Ferenczy, my old friend from Szentendre. I am always translating.

My whole justification codifies to one sentence: 'I have been taught.' I have no language here. Others will ache with this sunlight, and will rein in whatever the god of stillness is, out of pure movement that soars through my trained body like vertigo.

1899. June. Brisbane

Károly Pulszky in George Street

I seem in a mood for the unreal: even a street of shopkeepers is not real in a certain light. The light, here, is certain only of its memory of eucalyptus bark, shade-tree darkness with mosquitoes, tiers of hoop-pines, their particular stiffness.

Or the flash across water to the mangrove beds as a white heron arches. Yesterday, two pelicans.

Against the reality of birds in flight, or birds crushing waters into reflections and loops, these houses have no substance. The timber walls have forgotten wood, tin squinting all angles has surely forgotten earth and the underground storehouses of geology that were their origin.

HABERDASHERY   GREENGROCER   REAL ESTATE
THE BANK OF AUSTRALASIA

Men wear the garments of London or Vienna. Unreal, the burden of garments on men here. Gloves. The determination of hats. My mother would have defined all this with some presence. I find it hard, now, to be amused or amusing.

Is the business of selling, buying, spreading the rank butter of profit any more real than the business of sitting, looking, being amused or not amused?

My business was seeing. My reality was the clear world of vision, and it seemed specific. It was an ordering and serving, it was spread by fine artisans, strong with their hands.

In this climate the hands sweat in their gloves: this is called 'Winter'.

Brown ink, black ink, paper. What is *insurance*?

Yesterday someone before me in the bank brought in a bag of stone: gold. He exchanged it for paper. He will trade that paper for title deeds as if he were to become the possessor of land. Wild grasses carry seeds that clamber into wool and would burrow like worms into flesh. They will not be purchased. They will be owners forever or as long as forever matters.

Pods rattle among stained and torn leaves, grotesque. More than beautiful. Insects croak out, birds yelp, *beautiful, beautiful*.

At noon even horse-and-cart noise becomes apologetic, the noise of humans separates like glass splintering. I am lost in the mood of these times. How can only the grasslands be real? Europe has never seemed further. I have never felt more invisible.

1899. June 4th. Brisbane

Károly Pulszky remembers jokes

You heard the one about Diogenes, who went from place to place with a lamp in search of an honest man? When he reached Hungary he did not have to ask. He took one look then said: 'Here, take my lamp.'

It is not that the search is improbable.

Bitterness stings in the eye like oily smoke.

In my pocket, a linen handkerchief defines me: folded, precise, not to be used except as a measure of hiding secret evidence of process and decay. Two months, and each morning I still pursue old rituals. I am dried out, but still the habit instructs me: grooming, cuff links, trimming of the new beard, how else begin the routine of each day? Every act is a disguise.

I am surprised each time at the fluids within, at the fluids which surface.

We imagine ancestors to have acted like us. Aquincum, the capital of Pannonia Inferior (now Budapest) revealed, in my days as a student archaeologist, habits that were not inferior to the most elegant taste, to the most colonial assiduity. In colonial centres the forms are notoriously important.

It is not that the capitals, the centres change, but that the outposts must grip tight for fear of being spun off. There is no flexibility in Aquincum or in Brisbane. But there are salons here where the newest German philosophers are entertained (by proxy). Import and indent booksellers make a killing. Diogenes would have liked this point. Why did I never think of Budapest as an outpost? It was my centre.

Yet even houses can become ineffably strange; like my mother's descriptions of the American South, with 'open galleries on columns'. She wrote, also, about the burden of the heat, a winter clear as alpine air but curiously heavy, gripping the rim of the edge, the disc, the circle.

Here, also, the houses themselves are on stilts and pillars. The witch house on chicken legs, Baba Yaga.

Baba – Baby – why do I think of the Comtesse de Chevigné?

We love where we can.

It was not love. Appetite discards handkerchiefs, it has no time.

You heard the one about Diogenes with his lamp? He traded it in Plato's cave. In Plato's cave was Baba Yaga. A child was screaming, eyes stung by vision and by loss of vision and by shadows on the wall, firelit shadows that were the closest we come to explaining anything. But the child screamed only anger at the indifference of those who would not look even at shadows. I was that child.

The Comtesse de Chevigné is further away than Aquincum, where my studies began. They end in a place where even men are shadows. Sometimes, in this strong energy of sunlight I feel there is nothing, nobody here at all. Yet I am surrounded.

Károly Pulszky reads the Brisbane *Courier*

'London, June 1: In connection with the Dreyfus case, Major Esterházy has declared that the French Government tried to purchase the secrets and documents in his possession . . .'

The French Captain Dreyfus; his trial has come to haunt us all. His innocence turns into an accusation. Across the world, here, we await the terrible details of his martyrdom and the proof of this Major Esterházy's traitorous guilt. We expect no real reprieve for Dreyfus, on Devil's Island. They say that Major Esterházy dines superbly in Paris.

All Europe coils in on itself, a snake armlet crusted with jewels and venom. Why do I think my own case particular? The particular brings us all to ourselves. And to our senses, which we force to witness how despicable the body looks, exposed. Ask Monsieur Zola.

'Dreyfus, it is shown, knows several languages: crime. He works hard: crime. No compromising papers are found in his home: crime. He goes occasionally to his country of origin: crime. He endeavours to learn everything: crime. He is not easily worried: crime. He is worried: crime.'

Pulszky, it is shown, knows several languages: crime. He works hard: crime. No compromising papers are found in his home: crime. He endeavours to learn everything: crime, crime, crime.

He once believed in honour. He committed the crime of bringing dishonour to his family, to his wife, to his children. His crime is that he believes that. He is no Dreyfus, rigid with infallibility and a narrow belief in a narrow virtue. Dreyfus has only the virtue of knowing he is innocent. Life is more complex than that.

And yet, I am no traitor. I despise the so-called 'Count' Esterházy, the real traitor who lives it up in London, Paris,

Vienna. I despise his braggadaccio, his cupidity, his treachery, and most I despise his ignorance that without a shred of guilt allows the poor man, Dreyfus, still to linger alone in that terrible imprisonment, while all is revealed about the authorship of the very document used to condemn him. Esterházy – how Prince Esterházy himself must still be vitriolic to have his name flaunted in every paper of the world, even in Brisbane, by this Walsen-Esterházy of the brazen grin, this traitor turned informer, this distant relative who goes free while the victim is sacrificed.

I was never a traitor. I was nothing. I have become nothing, though once I was so full of quenchless zeal I could talk hours, without sleep – who needed sleep? I was on fire with the sense of possibility. It seems a life ago. I wake late, and am exhausted before I rise from my lumpy mattress.

Ask Esterházy – once, on the Eisenstadt Estate I paused by the Palladian Temple with the old Prince: we had been discussing Italian Primitives and whether his Canova *Princess Leopoldine* might not be included with the Esterházy Collection for my planned Gallery. The Prince demurred and then we talked on the nature of Art. 'It is a world of secrets,' I remember I said. 'Secrets and games. Like the Bertinelli grotesques on your courtyard architraves.' I was young and familiar, then. The Prince enjoyed my chatter. 'Or like the quartets of Josef Haydn: a balance into poise that unburdens us of time in the act of timing us.'

I believed in art. I thought that 'play' was the essential act in man, his defining quality, the magic to take all he beheld or intuited or feared and transmute it, as in glass, to hard, clear crystal. I was raked with broken bottles, later. Words become talons of glass. I believed in joy.

Man is defined by secrets and possession. The secrets are unspeakable. Possession gives the powerful means to refine their tortures as a fresh tang to their fortunes. Art is the plaything of princes.

I cannot believe that. Even the simplest of our folksongs refracts crystal:

> *Stork, stork, turtle-dove*
> *why are your feet bleeding?*
> *Turkish children cut them,*
> *Magyar children heal them*
> *with pipes, drums, reed violins.*

In the Turkish nights and nights and days of my exile and the Turkish silence of that three-month imprisonment, I had to hold to the belief in reed violins. I believed in nothing. I felt nothing. I became nothing. Yet I heard Magyar drums in my pulse-beat, Magyar pipes in my breathing. All sound was a form of suffocation, all silence was. Art is the way we become more than ourselves, and is a human quality. It is not held in locks by princes. Parliament-men may not understand what they lock themselves out of. That is decision, another human quality.

I had, myself, become locked out.

Tears on the back of a hand among hairs and the grit of road-dust become crystal for their moment in time. It is impertinence that we should think of art as immortality. It is the dream that each of us carries. I have failed that very dream.

Perhaps if I had the honour of a cypher, Dreyfus? Or the cunning of a Walsen-Esterházy? Perhaps if I had believed more fully in myself, but there is truth in every rumour, falsehood in the way we apprehend truth. Ask Zola, yes: ask Zola. He is dead, now.

When we returned to the Schloss, Prince Esterházy commended my enthusiasm. 'When you are older', he said, 'do not regret your rashness. I was in two minds whether to give you the Canova. This time you lost.'

And I walked to my barouche as if there had been something gained.

1899. June. Brisbane

Károly Pulszky accepts a job as canvasser for the A.M.P. Insurance Society

'Educated gentlemen from the Continent usually prefer to set up as photographers or teach music.'

I smiled.

'But your English is very commendable.'

I refrained.

'What is needed here, though, is the common touch. You understand? Not to intimidate, but to offer a partnership for Life.

58

To balance the policy with the poetry, as it were: death against security; tomorrow provided for; today's thrift yielding, if not a place in Heaven, some relief against mortgage and the harassments that render death painful. It is an art to induce concern, in those normally concerned only with their unconcern. You will learn the right jokes. I keep a list.'

These Englishmen, translated to the colonies, lose only their validity. I offered my credentials. They are excessive. It was, in the end, only the recommendation of Dr Hirschfeld here in Brisbane that induced them to 'take me on'. He wrote of my flair with languages and the untapped immigrant potential of Marburg, Petrie Bight, and of Silesian vignerons at Myrtletown. The Doctor lives with unplanned tragedies and frugal Germans without foresight. I live only with aftersight. A gentleman might do less.

Outside, my folder already stained with sweat, I passed a boy dousing his handkerchief in a horse trough then mopping his brow. Until he spoke I thought the face some urchin recognised by Caravaggio. After, I knew.

'Dr Hirschfeld tells me you once dealt in canvas, Mr Pulszky. As a canvasser your art will be to apply the stroke of gloss that makes the apple tempting. I wish you good luck.'

In his hand I recognised the softness of my own. I do not believe he understood the extent of our deceit.

> Miss Tessa Pulszky
> C/- Mme Emilia Markus
> Royal Hotel
> Budapest V
> HUNGARY

Brisbane, 4th June, 1899

My dear Tessa!

By the time you receive this letter your exams will be over, and I hope they went well. But if the result was not as desired, not as good as you were hoping for, don't be discouraged. The reason for this is that in the lower classes you were not sufficiently industrious and thorough when studying the basics, and one can not make up for this later. This should be a lesson to you ... Now, if you wish to become a singer, and you have the right voice, don't imagine that the theoretical study is unimportant, and do not neglect it. A thorough all-round musical education, and even the history of literature and other subjects seemingly far removed from the profession – to neglect mastering these will make you feel sorry later, just as the lack of basic mathematics made you feel during high school studies. Above all, be serious about music – theory, counterpoint, and composition, even if they seem boring in the beginning; without a thorough knowledge of these, you might become an excellent singing or piano-playing machine, but never a true artist ... you should get used to serious literature, otherwise you'll find that your education is incomplete, that what occupies the interest of truly worthy people – men and women – will bore you, because you don't understand it; and so you'll be a stranger in the company of valuable well educated people. Believe me, in time you'll be bitterly sorry if you don't follow my advice in this regard ...

However much you do enjoy other people's company, however much they like you, however much you are having a good time there, don't ever let yourself be alienated from your home; your mother and sister must always stay nearest to your heart, and now that you are a big girl, I know that you feel and understand how much you may help mother in every way, and how useful you can be in the upbringing of Romola, so that she should turn to you with all her troubles, knowing that you'll be glad to help.

I will probably leave here. Don't write until I write with a new address.

God bless you my dear daughter, many kisses from your very loving father
Charlie

Dr Eugen Hirschfeld invites Károly Pulszky to his dinner table

— My guess would have been – what would it have been? That lean bearing, the carriage small but like wire – I should have said someone in high office, but not inordinate: a Government post, say, with just enough supervision to be intolerable. How is that? Comptroller of Customs? Registrar of the new university (you see, I keep au courant, even with Budapest). Yes, very close, I can read everything. Language itself is more often a disguise, though like garments, yet another clue to the mystery – have you read the new English tales of mystery and detection? Sir Arthur Conan Doyle?

— Dr Hirschfeld, I think you uncanny. And a most energetic host. I swore myself to silence. You are in danger of destroying that resolution – like my resolution against wine and the flesh of animals. Indeed, against any indulgence of the senses, or the mind.

— We make our own boundaries. And our own prisons. I see men in cages walk past me in full sunlight – men who do not see this a particular place of abundance. They walk through Eden itself shackled and in chains of their own making. I believe they call it exile, generally, it is a very common term. It means nothing. Or at most, a lack of imagination. What we have before us in Brisbane is an open slate, a page still blank, on which we have the power to inscribe the prescriptions that the future must follow. I call that a rare power. That was the reason I became a naturalised citizen in '93. I came to this country with £20, no more. Now, in my thirties, I have the prospects of a baronet.

— Nothing I see here convinces me the past is alive. I cannot live cut off from my sources.

— Not so, not so. It is the future that waits on the page. I confess I am impatient. But it needs only a handful of visionaries . . .

— I am not one.

— Think of the potential! You can pluck from the past what

61

you will or what you need. Then sift and filter it to your own vision. You must understand the opportunities. Do not neglect to seize and take hold. You must shake off your mood of abandonment.

– In Budapest I had power, and the possibilities. That is past.

– Good God man, nothing is past. You must attend to my meaning. What do you know of this colony? Nothing. You still sulk in Hungary. This area is extraordinary. Have you noted the local inhabitants, the aboriginal people? Even with the corruption of flour, sugar and cheap alcohol, what upright bearing! Strong frames, virile posture. Examining the early records I have noted the observations of Oxley and the first explorers: abundance of seafood always, native fruit and berries in abundance. Have you discovered the macadamia? The locals call it 'bopple nut'. Excellent, more than excellent – superb. Or the nut of the Bunya pine in season? Were I an agronomist not a physician I assure you I would produce and export. As it is, I am already determined to exploit the local farming potentials. Wealth is all about us for the plucking. Have you seen the astounding fleece of the Australian merino sheep? There is a stud at Rosenthal on the upland Downs where Silesian merinos were introduced from the Esterházy flock; they were crossed with McArthur's Camden Billy . . .

– On my father's estate, as a youth I was entranced at the shearing, we had the same merinos, out of the Esterházy flock. My dear Hirschfeld, your innocent enthusiasm and cupidity wounds deeply, but in ways you cannot understand.

– But sir, sir, you owned merino flocks? I cannot believe your luck. I think you were intended for Australia.

– I once thought I was intended for Italy, the Italy of four hundred years back. I am destined for exile – exile from dreams, from homeland, family, and the one real edifice my training equipped me for.

– You must beware the most common confusion here. For 'exile' do you mean 'inertia'? Well, then?

– For 'exile' I mean the self, abandoned. Silence. No joy or communication. I came from a culture where we were incessant in the expression of shared discourse. In a sense, everything was public, almost from birth my whole life was public, was a sort of theatre. Remove the sounding board – and the fiddle will not even play for itself.

– Beethoven composed in his own head, in complete deafness.

62

– I have learned, then, the genius of Beethoven. And the lack of my own.

– Aha. Now you begin. You are not a boy now, setting yourself up against models. There is no headmaster over you, no stern father. That is the release possible in a new place. What you tell me – not in words – is that the loss of position, of security, and perhaps of a certain power, has undone you. And yet, you are here, at my table, alive, in mid life, you could be edged out into wit, even pleasure, with just a little effort. Undone? Buttons, sir! I do not think Beethoven was clever with buttons, either. Or with coffee, or women, or the laundering of linen. So you did seek vision, eh? Or felt you held it? That is what you tell me.

– I was Director of the Hungarian National Art Museum. I created my own vision. I assure you, sir, my achievement there will outlast my enemies.

– Good. Good.

– This is not self-mockery. I began my collection from nothing. From the erratic concoctions of the Esterházys, and they did indeed assemble some treasures. Though as you know, Hungary's greatest treasures from the Renaissance flowering at the court of Matthias Corvina were destroyed in the Turkish invasion. What I began with was a random assemblage. In the Esterházy's Dutch genre pieces, or some eighteenth-century masters, and of course a few gems like the Rafael *Madonna*, there were gems indeed. But in four years I imposed a larger overview and a balance. It was more than filling in gaps. I created a Gallery. Then I added a whole wing of sculpture, wondrous things, some of them. And the frescoes – I even managed the feat of transporting a dozen and more large Renaissance frescoes from Italy back to the Museum. That is without parallel. All it meant was I became a target for slander, and in the end, an entire campaign against me was successful. Oh yes, it succeeded. You would not believe how many months the snide journalists made a living with cheap sensation and unconfirmed rumour, smut, lies – worse than lies, political deceit!

– So you fled?

– I was convicted. No, I'll not go into it. The charges, to be specific, were withdrawn. After two years. And then, only as a sort of technicality. I have the comfort of knowing I have no criminal record. I had, instead, a collapse. Enough.

– Still, what you have told me pleads an essential innocence.

63

— I think I was guilty. No, not to conscious embezzlement, not to 'misappropriation of funds' as they termed it. Those charges were not the real charges. I was charged with breaking permitted boundaries. I had a vision, and I rushed to attain it. I had a life-style – and I did not hesitate to pursue it. It was a model of its kind, it involved sharing, and energy and stretching oneself to the limit and then beyond. You've no idea how much a challenge that was to others. They said I was mad. My own wife, at first, lured me on with this ideal, we were in it together. We created our own continent . . .

— Ah yes, yes there was a wife of course . . .

— In fifteen years we sought to create a universe in the heart of Budapest; we were a court, a dynasty, we set out to create our own life as a work of art . . .

— Ruskin and Pater . . . She of course encouraged you?

— She impelled me. She inspired me. I think it was her focus: of course I had attained, earlier, before marriage, great expertness in my field. I prepared the Hungarian exhibit of folk design for the Paris Exposition when I was still a student, I published books on it, I was an archaeologist . . .

— Australia. You have great talents. You must not waste them, and certainly not here, where talent and leadership are so urgently needed. Do not undervalue your talents, they are not entirely yours. Think of them as a trust. We have needs here, I assure you, and you must consider them. Remember inertia. You should plot them as an exercise, a project for the interim, a sort of minor challenge. You have heard we are just beginning a new art gallery in Brisbane? And you, here, with your experience!

— To think of art, now, is to think of my exile. To think of sculp-ture, is to remember charges and rumour. To remember my skills is to have them turn upon me like knives.

— You are selfish. You have always been selfish.

— How can you say that? You know nothing of me.

— I say that as observation. We write our own histories in the face and the hands and the slump or the lilt. By our fortieth year we are a dictionary. Add another five years and the document is an encyclopaedia. But when I say that, you must understand I believe selfishness is a first prompt to growth. Self-Reliance, sayeth Emerson.

— I am a socialist.

64

Károly Pulszky remembers the statue of Christ by Andrea del Verrocchio in his father's house, Budapest

Some things you accept by growing up alongside them. They are you because each turn in you is measured with their proportion. Some things turn into you. They foreshadow you but cannot tell you. This is not prophecy, it is act that only later must be fulfilled.

In my father's house was the large Verrocchio *Imago Pietatis* in terracotta. Christ in the long hole of suffering. He opens his wound. His eyes look from the other side of the earth, from so far off no language can hold together. In my youth they sought me out. Hours I would meditate. I knew everything soon enough – I mapped the dead city, Aquincum, on the banks of the Danube, I was an archaeologist of every age but my own, and then later I became a connoisseur of art, of the past, turning the keys easily, so eager I would have broken any lock. I became so busy I forgot silence. Those first hours of stillness became, like hours of boredom through adolescence, pools not sought for after.

They catch me up. I know I must learn that stillness.

I twitch, I ache in the neck, the wrist, the muscles of the jaw. Why should Verrocchio follow me here? I am not the same. I have no wound to point out. Yet twenty shredding quills grind into me. Nothing visible. Pain holds your shoulder thus, the head thus, in precise lines. The Verrocchio head, even the fall of hair. The eyes half closed. Most, when half closed in concentration. Even teeth echo pain, the muscles around the lips, they are traitors. Pain has a great quality of silence, it steps in. At a certain point, all you are is pain.

That artist knew this. My father bought the work when I was a boy, it made me dream of Florence. I do not know why he took it, later, to his Museum. He was Director, so it was perhaps strategy, his donation. He spoke of the statue's nobility.

I only saw suffering.

65

I came to call it self-indulgent, the Christian safety in weakness and perhaps a power to coerce through poverty. I felt rich.

Later, I felt rich indeed, power waited on me. My father approved. My apartment in the Academy was the talk, and the envy, of Budapest. I collected rich things, they said, and the crowning prize was my wife.

My father never approved enough. I hated him on that morning they removed my Christ of the open wound. I had to learn. Very well, I let others stare at it. I became disaffected.

My father was a man of action, his energy prodigious. How could I admit the prophecy? It meant stillness. I have run 18,000 miles. He has blessed me and I know I have failed. The Christ of Verrocchio knew that.

To survive – to be resurrected – is to live in that failure, to live with it interminably. Christ points to the wound but his face is describing the loss from God. Nothing matters. The pain is not physical, it is no spear thrust. The words on the Cross were true words. Even in death, the forsaken son is not free.

Károly Pulszky's dream

My stag hooves clatter over Széchény Bridge. They strike sparks. They bound away from the fires of sparks. My stag hooves echo back across Pest.

In the caverns of new Renaissance palaces stucco and mortar have caught their own sound. It rips sharply, hoof-blade. In the Academy of Sciences it rips down the first floor. Not my Gobelin tapestries nor my carpets can smother it. It fills each corridor and laughs at my wife, painted life-size on the clever door to her dressing-room. It is part of my nerve; my nerves scream under the strain. It is my own doing, my own hooves. In the caverns of noise my hooves are true also.

In the ears of the city they are linotype machines. I am hurled like lead ingots to become rigid print. Newspapers are my own hounds, baying and panting, the sound of linotype their hot breath behind. My city turns into a forest, there must be a passageway. I spring out. My streets become tracks. The forest remains linotype. I called to you mother. I heard my father cry out my name. I have none.

I called again to you, mother, you had become a pale hind. Hounds licked your blood fever, your dead rigid carcass. My father bucked off as they tore. A son should not see how his father is ripped in the underbelly, how entrails are gulped while still hot, how the hounds, my own, tear with blood-lust. A son should not see his mother dead.

A mother should not burn up and demand his helplessness, the panic of being the terrible untouched one, the witness, the survivor. The curse waited upon Actaeon.

Sparks out of iron bridges.

My stag hooves break off. Eighteen thousand miles. To know the world a pack gorged on live bodies is to grow antlers. To look upon the unknowable goddess of fever is to grow antlers, is to sharpen antlers. They ache above me, are part of me. Wherever they rub they rip off their velvet to reveal blades. That place becomes part of the spirit of antlers.

My mother, taking notes, says these trees are different. Curious.

My father explains cranial slopes of the Australian Aborigine. It is as if my dream were not important here. As if the burden in bone from my head were part of my own fever, not theirs. They indulge my old nightmare. They back away. It is click of dog claws. Dogs are crossing Széchény Bridge. It is the gasp of breath. Tell it to me, my mother says, but I cannot.

Tell it to me. And again, tell it.

I am fourteen years old. Again she insists. Sobbing because she is dead. Tell it, tell your dream to me now.

My sister scalding, dying, my mother pale with the ache of first typhus fever, and knowing. The fever consumes everything, when will it come? Why am I spared to suffer still? Must I witness everything? Mother. Mother, are you listening? I will tell. I will tell everything.

I have antlers of true sharp blades. I will not be caged in. My stag hooves clatter over Széchény Bridge.

Mother, when I come into your room my hooves will cut your hot goddess flesh away from the bone. There is no father. I am alone.

Excerpt from the newspaper
Budapesti Hirlap

We hope that Károly Pulszky will recover from his serious neurosis by the time the budget discussions come up. The amount granted in last year's budget (372,460 florins) was for the purpose of augmenting the collection of Old Masters for the future Museum of Fine Arts. According to our reporter, Károly Pulszky is so ill that he can not be treated at home, and will be transferred today or tomorrow to one of the mental hospitals.

The fact that the seriously ill patient's wife, the celebrated actress Emilia Markus, appeared in the parliamentary gallery and visibly enjoyed the debate about theatres makes this news the more unexpected and surprising.

Today, Madame Emilia Markus, her eyes red from crying, told our reporter: 'Since his return from Italy, my husband fell into deep apathy, a sort of melancholy; in contrast with last summer, when he was very excited and nervy. He didn't care about anything, he lay in bed for days with his eyes fixed on one spot. He scarcely recognized the children and myself. Lately he had such fits that we had to hide every possible weapon. He tried to commit suicide a few days ago with a revolver. He did that several times before. Dr Kresz and Dr Plosz decided to admit him to hospital. He had a severe attack yesterday. I offered to take two months off work and look after him myself, but they said this is not safe.'

This afternoon a consultation by five doctors took place at the Pulszky home, at the request of the family. During the thorough examination Pulszky took hardly any notice, his only answer to questions has been: 'Everything is all right! Leave me alone!'

According to a signed statement the doctors declared that they found him completely apathetic and insensible in certain parts of the body. They claim to have found several other symptoms typical of mental disorder. The statement concluded that Pulszky was a danger to himself and the public, and he must be urgently admitted to an asylum. The discussion lasted from 4 p.m. to 11 p.m. One doctor left without signing . . .

On the 27th December last year, we had information about the sale at the Scarpa Gallery, Milan, of a man's portrait by Piombo (believed formerly to be by Rafael). The Countess Chevigné paid 135,000 francs for this. It is suggested that the real buyer is the Director of the National Gallery, Károly Pulszky, who escorted the Countess. The painting has been painted over. It's questionable if anything was left underneath from the original painting. Such a price is far too high for a repainted painting. Károly Pulszky has not commented to our reporter on this bit of news.

Part III: Portrait of Emilia Markus

'This is how one fares if one comes from a far country.'

The actress Kornelia Prielle writes to a friend about a soirée at the Pulszky apartment in the Academy of Sciences, Budapest

The milieu in which Charlie has placed his little wife by his expert taste and extravagant lavishness is something else again! I had heard about it, but it surpassed my imagination. I have never seen anything like this. Compared with the homes of our aristocrats or palaces abroad, I have never found so much luxury and eccentricity for just two people.

And they seemed to revel in it! Emilia Markus, is indeed the 'blonde wonder'. Her hair is extraordinary – it seems to sparkle. I could not keep my eyes from it, while she was in the room. When she was out of the room, then the furnishings and accessories were giddying. Did you know her portrait in the costume of Desdemona has been painted by János Temple. But it has been placed in one of the door frames of the apartment. Emilia – Emmy, she is called by everyone – at one stage early in the evening disappeared, just after telling us the story of the painting and its execution. She intended playing a trick on us: for a few minutes later, when conversation had moved to some other topic, she quietly opened that door and stood in the place of the portrait, and wearing her Desdemona costume.

Charlie pointed, and as we turned, the 'painting' stepped forward, out of its frame. I tell you, the moment was quite magical, almost disturbing. We applauded.

What makes the salon outstanding, though, is neither the opulence nor the curiosity of the scattered objects, its endless surprises and interest; nor the company itself, though that comprised the cream of the theatre world, the intellectual elite and a fair sprinkling of notable political figures. No, it was the aura of the Pulszky couple, our hosts. Emilia has such a wonderful, expressive face and mouth, she exudes warmth. While Charlie burns with a glitter, his energy is enormous and seems to have pared down his willowy figure like a racehorse or some wild stag. Together, they complement each other, and I am sure bring out new qualities and insights in each other. I have it for certain that Emmy's wide interest and knowledge in art matters derives entirely from dear Charlie, while his whole energy, which otherwise might dissipate in feckless schemes, seems focused by her powers of concentration, that wonderful ability of hers to master a part completely and turn it into herself.

I had the opportunity to watch them together later in the evening, after the meal (which of course was superb, right down to the exquisite Japanese dolls which decorate the placemarks. Mine I have kept). Their tenderness together touched me hugely. Emmy cast her eyes on him for just one moment and he turned immediately to her. I think he might have swept to his knees before her without compunction – and the gesture, in him, would have seemed in perfect accord.

As it was, he found her a chair and for a few moments they conversed quietly together as if there were nobody else in the room. As she spoke to him she stroked his dinner-jacket gently. His dark, sparkling eyes consumed her. There was a noticeable hush, though we all recovered quickly, perhaps embarrassed at seeming to be onlookers. I left after that.

There are some couples whose happiness together is almost indecent, you wish for a flaw to show, some crack to open up and reveal them human. Not only human, but as horrible as you are yourself, deep down. The Pulszkys seem to glide through an enchanted world, one that has none of our own gritty reality. When the doors of their fairy palace do open, I fear the shock will be very great.

Emilia Markus returns from a performance of Dumas's *The Lady of the Camellias* to discover her daughter Romola with a fever

But you are burning up! My poor little flower, when did this come upon you, and where has Tessa been that you did not call her? Tell me? Tell it to me. There there, I am home now and you have no cause for worry. Is your throat sore? Tell me, is it swollen? Let me feel if it is swollen.

Now you are settled, I feel you are cooler already but I will sit here still with this damp cloth and mop your brow. That was the fever passing, it flowed out with your perspiration, so in the morning you will be able to feel well again. But you must be careful, and take lemon.

I will read to you. You must try to sleep.

Here, one of these old legends from that book by Charlie's mother, I know you enjoy those. Are you settled properly, and will not interrupt? Good girl.

'When in the thirteenth Century the Tartars, led by their chief, Batu Khan, invaded Hungary, and King Béla was forced to flee from the disastrous battle at the Sajo, despair seized upon the Hungarians. Many had fallen on the field, still more were butchered by the faithless enemy; some sought escape, others apathetically awaited their fate.'

Do you know a word like 'apathetically'? Good girl.

I will continue, yes of course. You look so pale, so pretty and so pale.

'Amongst these was a nobleman, who lived retired on his property, distant from every highroad. He possessed fine herds, stately horses, rich cornfields, and a well-stocked house, built but recently for the reception of his wife, who now for two years had been its mistress.'

Imagine something like our old apartment, very rich and full of loved treasures. No, I should not invoke that, I thought it might make the story more vivid for you.

'The disheartening account of misfortune reached this secluded place and its peaceful lord·was horrified ... suddenly a Tartar on his steed galloped into the court. The Hungarian bounced from his seat, ran to meet his guest, and said: "Tartar, thou art my lord; I am thy servant; all thou seest is thine. Take what thou fanciest; I do not oppose thy power; command – thy servant obeys."

'The Tartar impatiently sprang from his horse, entered the house and cast a careless glance on all the precious objects around. His eye was fascinated by the brilliant beauty of the lady of the house, who appeared tastefully attired to greet him here ... the Tartar seized her without a moment's hesitation, and unheedful of her shrieks, swung her upon his saddle, and spurred away ... the nobleman·was thunderstruck, but he recovered and hastened to the gate. He heaved a sigh and exclaimed with deep commiseration: "Alas, poor Tartar!".'

Well, an amusing tale, I was taught a slightly different version, as a child. It concerned a Hungarian nobleman with a city palace where h kept his lovely bride. But then, as a small child I lived in the country, before my father died and I moved into my uncle's household. What do you think the Tartar did when he discovered what he had got?

Why, that's very clever, little Romola, I think I agree with you; the nobleman, from all accounts was indeed a dull man, and didn't know how to treat his lovely wife, you are quite right.

Do you think the Tartar would be more romantic and considerate? No, do not twist my ring like that, the snake chafes me when you do that. Of course I wear it. It was your father's; I will wear it forever.

I think the Tartar would have been more gallant. And besides, the lady would be clever and know how to twist *him* around her little finger. *He* was dashing, and exciting, but also, clearly, another fool. The moral of the story, then, is plain. These men. They dress themselves into rôles and positions and lose themselves in them. It's only when they step outside, or are wrenched out, or pushed, or forced ...

I won't kiss you. Your little eyes still sparkle and burn. Here.
For this once you may wear the snake-jewel ring. Charlie said it
brings the wearer luck. Look into the jewel and see if you can read
your fortune. Or mine.

No, not tonight. Shall I read another tale? In the morning, if
you like, and are feeling up to it, I will allow you to brush my
hair.

I know your father would have stayed with you all night, yes,
but he is no longer here and you are a big girl now. And I, truly,
I am so exhausted. Sometimes the burden of continuing is more
than I can bear. To look ahead is to know the weight of it. Each
day, each night, that is the way to endure, as you must endure
your father's absence. After all, distance is not always personal.

I bet that Lady tricked the Tartar at the very first stop for his
horse to rest. Do you think she was home with her husband that
very night? Serve him right.

1899. Budapest

Emilia Markus remembering

The look of women, dissatisfied over chocolate-walnut crêpes in
a restaurant, or wiping fat from lips, fingering crystal. I discern
of late these women everywhere, my age.

He was always restless.

Look of unappeased hunger – I had not been aware before how
eyes betray the bed, cold sheets, the perfunction of middle age
and the first webs across the belly, that womb-spider waiting to
spin. Women grow angry with appetite.

He was always away.

Mari Jaszai today, in rehearsal, her 'understanding'. I reminded her of her old infatuation with Gustav Mahler. I cannot
stop this viciousness. My children suffer. Mari and her new con-
ductor dazzling us in his opera-house till we were flung singing
into the streets. We are not comfortable with demands that search
us out and insist, and keep on insisting.

My husband was always searching.

This Mahler, his symphony appalled. Fierce anger from such
a small man, the instruments turned into each other, the music

77

into animals mocking the hunter in us. The hidden ache should have forewarned me. I was to know everything.

My husband mocked enemies.

At the end of each movement, applause. After the performance young Mahler was avoided. He was dismissed shortly, they say his Wagner in Vienna is breathtaking. My husband was ironic over him in Florence, Mahler had not even seen the Uffizi. They walked to the hills together and talked politics.

My husband was born into politics. It destroyed him.

Hunger of Mari Jaszai, always studying new rôles, hunger of Mahler, night after night forcing us to his vision. They say I have a hungry mind. Thirst of my own poor Charlie, scooping art works from Italy. Hunger of audiences for my gift of the milky ache in comedy, for updraughts of life-force in tragedy. And this last hunger, the knowledge of appetite unslaked forever.

He was restless. He failed me.

I cannot forgive the slander of friends. I cannot forgive the look from under parasols, appraising eyes, hawk eyes, badger eyes, rodent. I cannot forgive the blind dazed look of my husband after three months' captivity. That drained off his mockery and his fine stance. I cannot forgive the loss, in my own needs it has turned to deceit, it has turned me accuser, turned me with appetite into the others.

He was always accusing me.

I cannot forgive.

I cannot acknowledge how much of myself he gave me, how much of myself he took.

Emmy sings (1)

I loved you as my idol.
I loved you as bright shafts of colour.
I loved you as two gentle hands.
I loved you as laughter and again laughter.
I loved you as someone leading towards a bright hill.
I loved you as someone who would pause because there were celandines or old-man's-beard.
I loved you because you could pause, then, in the shade.

I loved you because you sprinted before me to the top of
  Géllert Hill;
    because you quoted Petrarch to me then, and it meant
      everything.

I loved to catch your neat figure ahead of me in the Véci.
I loved the back of your neck.
I loved the way your eyes glowed. They were ponds in a forest
  but for me you made them tokaji.
I loved that.

I loved to hear your voice calling from another room,
  'Emmy! Where is my Emmy!'
I loved to hear your voice say my name. I loved you for your
  voice and the way it enshrined my name.
I loved to know you meant it. You meant it.
I loved to know you.
I never knew you. But in everything, you meant it.

Emmy sings (2)

You knew when the theatre was closed
  that I grew unprotected.
You knew when my costume was off
  that I lost three parts of my presence.
You knew how to colour the void;
  how to see in the dark of my shadow;
  how to wake other cities and countries in me,
  how to enchant me into a meadow.

I was brittle as glass and as light as glass. You knew.
I was a goblet that danced in the light. You knew that too.
You knew I had storerooms of rich brocade,
  larders and baskets of banquet fare,
  cellars and turrets and battlements,
  gallery and loggia and deep corridors,
  avenues flanked with linden in bloom;
you knew where the map of my future would be
and you knew that together we'd learn the key.

We learned the key.
When the key was opened you knew I was free.
The debt is something I'll never repay.
You knew.
On my stage I salute. It has all come true.
All our worlds were the same. That's how we grew.
Now I'm alone.
I have known you.
Now I am alone.
I will pull through.
Ahead are the things
that you never knew.
It was not I who destroyed you.
Has my knowledge destroyed you?
Which of us guessed that? which of us feared that?
Which one knew?

Emmy sings (3)

You were here last night in a dream.
The river had flooded its banks
till the Margaret Isle was under
and you said: I will come home.

You were here in the night in my dream.
All the chestnut trees in flower
were sighing with pollen and bees
and you said: I am coming home.

You were somewhere within my dream
and the hills were hazy with summer.
'O I cannot bear it alone',
you said, 'I must see you
and come home.'

And you came home to my dream.
But the room was our old home
and the Danube has flooded and gone
and your body had lost its name
my love,
your body had lost its name.

Károly Pulszky strikes matches

Two boxes of matches: why do I think of Emmy? Some people rise like pure flame into the upthrust of energy, some people are held between thumb and forefinger like sticks. Emmy was pure flame. I believed that, hardly knowing that flame draws into itself every impurity, fuels itself from the resource of pure appetite only. Appetite is only a way of taking, commanding, commandeering, it is consuming itself with demands.

You do not think of that.

I was drawn impossibly to that. The yearning, at the hollow centre of impure burning. My wife, in the theatre, on her stage, dragged from an audience pure tribute, she may rejoice in that. She will be relearning again and again what its process is, somewhere.

Budapest is a long way off.

The stone cast up into the air comes down to earth. The match twig will be returned to some element. Nothing is forgotten entirely. *Again and again your son will return to you, my land, I am yours in great anger and defection*. O too honest Pétofi.

Imprint of thumb and forefinger. Emmy, if you had in your heart believed in me you would have understood timber, twig, friction. It was pure flame I held, caught up in a halo, an aura, the giant stride of a stone cast up high, catapulting, soaring across lands to the dealers in Florence, Milano, Torino – my sight was pure flame, I gathered in sculpture, carvings, canvases, I had it in me to create Budapest in my own image, to make a National Gallery all of Europe would flock to. I was powerful as an Esterházy but with more discernment.

Yes, I know how you consumed them in your performance. I stood in the wings, many times and thought: she is mine.

I too had power. Why does even marriage end in rivalry?

I am tossed away a hundred times. In my unfaithfulness you were the centre. 'Will you cover my body with your shroud?' Remember we once sang that together and the salon became so still we were embarrassed, we laughed to break the silence. You were a jeweled armlet and I was pure gold, that was what our youth declared before them, that mere audience, a gathering of candles.

I fret for the children. I am glad nobody can see me. Honour is the one thing even a matchstick has, in its own fashion. Craft needs no apology.

Everything is forgotten entirely. I was a buyer of other men's masterworks. I was a stone ricochetting across water. I was, at most, a dealer in insurances, a gambler with life and with art.

When you take a new lover there will be ash and fingerprints. A man's sense of self-honour is the last thing he abandons. And then, utterly.

Károly Pulszky takes off his clothes

Nobody takes off all his clothes. Nobody turns the other way. Nobody is embarrassed and is ashamed to admit it. Nobody himself has never looked at himself, has never looked at his wife.

I looked at my wife with such heat it dried out the fluid of my eyes, it scalded my skin so it flaked, it made my fingers dry when I wanted unguents of them.

I looked in the desire of unguents at my wife naked; I took my privilege. I claimed her. Why can we not be close to the focus we share? Why can I never be close? I triumphed.

I am in exile.

In the end I arrive at a bare room made of boards that join with each other. 'Tongue and groove' they call it, but the rough boys give it a different name. Timber here partakes of phallic thrust, female cleft. The new cities are frank.

We were frank, in that first slap of the door and claim of a betrothal ring. Later, even more urgently.

Before we knew urgency we knew urgency. Before we became desperate there was desperation between us – tracks along the skin, tugs into muscle, wrench and distended tongue, anxiety.

I am naked now. It was a delight to her and I was too long before I acknowledged it: I was a delight to her.

It was a delight to be something like a carcass, estranged from the comforts, out in the open, opening each other out; I even believed I might become vulnerable and we explored everything together. Each other.

As it became desperate we exchanged, we negotiated, we were exchange, exchanging, changing ...

I was abashed when she leant down, took me into her mouth, then became imperious as if she were hungry for protein (I flinch to declare my science) and in the return I am still abashed to recall I moved even further as if desperate into her, my tongue into her welling drinking deeper gushing in a taste for her nothing prepared me for.

It was never repeated.

My tongue still aches for the drip and flood that made taste a white wakening that made me taste something like nothing exists in any other context.

I am forced on by absence, by hate, by love, by thought that is relentless in recreating me and the details of nakedness, now that even nakedness is absent forever.

... her muscles tight in the opening, her will greater than anything possible and my own lust dispersed, limp, vanished into my tongue and the greater urgency than consideration merely of the singular member – how justify that? How justify that? It was marvellous.

It opened nothing.

Later, naked, we were considering each other. We could not explain ourselves. I pursed at her appetite knowing it a vortex, not taken again, not any second time.

I will remember it forever.

She was not open, she opened to caverns, she was muscle, bone, muscle. She demanded feeling. Nothing of feeling exists in someone who demands. We were intolerably anxious, in our time. We were anatomy, bone, muscle. I once tasted her depths she once gulped the most strange part of me. We both discovered the dryness of appetite.

Brisbane, 9th June, 1899

Dear Emma!

I hope you receive this letter not in Pest, but somewhere in the country, at a spa or resort, where rest and good air will again restore your health completely.

Your last letter from 21st April has reassured me in many ways. Although the fact that again this season you had to perform while being unwell, and your voice is affected again, is worrying. Still, it's important that your pleasure in life has started to return. I notice this from your writing and am very pleased.

Naturally the financial worries are still pressing, and prevent you from being able to enjoy the successes you are achieving by so much effort and self-sacrifice. But I notice that you try with sufficient seriousness to conquer them, slowly ...

Your rôle is doubly difficult in a distressing situation brought about by my mistakes. Only because of your great qualities and because your daughters are found likeable by everybody, will the community back home eventually forget my dark memory. That you are starting to achieve this already, that the false situation for the poor children is slowly improving, takes the edge off the bitterness I felt for their suffering caused by my deeds.

The more I reflect on the past, the more I understand that the basic cause of our many sufferings was brought about by my weakness; if fifteen years ago – when not even the slightest serious disharmony disturbed our happiness – I could have been more forceful with myself and with you – all that has happened would not have ensued.

Of course I can never restore the lost balance, neither in the outside situation, nor in my private life.

So don't ever allow your self-confidence to diminish by misunderstanding the memories and accusing yourself.

... In bringing up the children try to assure that they will not become selfish and capricious. Too much love and pampering made both of them liable to selfishness. I know that for you, being so occupied and claimed by your rôles, it's often much easier to grant than reject even their unreasonable wishes, to save yourself from troublesome unpleasant hours . . .

I hope better circumstances will surround Romola's development. The storms of your life have passed and the memories of the sad events of her childhood will fade by the time she grows up; but guard her from being spoiled . . . I only want to warn you, don't punish or scold them with excessive anger and vehemence for small mistakes, neglects and clumsiness – as it formerly used to happen sometimes. At such times they only see the injustice of the exaggeration and not their own wrongdoing, and spite is born instead of the wish for improvement. I know that such things happen as a result of your nervousness and it does distress you more than them. That's why you must doubly avoid it.

You know best what a disaster it is when mother and daughter do not understand each other, when sisters are not each other's closest, best friends; you know that the lack of this is irreplaceable and when there is sufficient unity and sincerity what great help and support these are in life's difficulties.

Tessa will be so grown up in one or two years' time that she might become not only your daughter but also your friend. Nobody has been, unfortunately, that before.

Try to ensure that Romola shall become yours and also Tessa's friend despite the difference in their ages; that they should be quite honest towards each other, believe me this is only possible if the sincerity is mutual.

Don't ever forget your example will even more influence them than your words. You would try in vain to hide part of your life from them; therefore don't do anything you would want to keep secret from them . . .

Don't take offence for my writing these things. Though I feel and believe it quite purposeless. But I am prompted by my love for you and my anxiety for your future and tranquillity. It's all that's still worthy in me.

I don't know when I'll be able to write again. I am not succeeding here at all, though I am making every effort. I still cannot achieve any results. In a few days I shall probably go further north, where postal connections might not be certain . . .

I am so far away from you and I can hardly encourage myself with the hope of ever seeing you all again. Of course, at my age one would need great luck to achieve new results, for one's diminishing talents to assert themselves. Therefore I am not bitter about the lack of success, I am not searching for the reasons in the injustice of people, or in adverse circumstances; I must atone for my own mistakes – and this knowledge keeps me calm.

I try to uphold till the end the possibility of restitution for my offences against you and others; if this stops, then I am not to be pitied, I would be the first to refuse sympathy.

I think I have always striven in the past (though the opposite of this has eventuated) to make others happy, and have not vied for my own advantage and happiness. Now I could possibly do something to your advantage by being able to perish, as I can not actively better your position. But this is the secret of the future.

Whatever fate might bring, be always aware that your behaviour in the past difficult situation, your lovingly fulfilled duty to the children, is the only happiness and contentment I have had in these desolate and sad months, and makes it possible for me to face whatever follows, with calm determination.

Many kisses to all three of you; do love each other as I love you all wherever my destiny will take me; and if life's adversity would make you resent each other, remember how much this will hurt me wherever I'd be. Only the knowledge of your unity can give me peace – by now the only thing I am yearning for.

God bless you dear Emma, think of me without bitterness.
Charlie

1899. June 10th. Brisbane

Dr Eugen Hirschfeld considers the case of Károly Pulszky

What a preternaturally cold place, the Brisbane Morgue. I have identified the corpse. Case concluded. So. I can file another manilla folder. It almost goes with the ones marked: 'Do not destroy – case interesting.' But I do not know. Who will be remembered? Who forgotten? There is hardly enough in the Pulszky affair to go on.

A formal interview; a rather pleasant, garrulous meal together where we ended as I recall with some rather convivial songs at the piano. One evening at the German Club.

I wonder, though, at the clues. I clearly did not grasp all the connections.

That man had enough flair, wit, intelligence to master five professions, seven languages, four continents, any number of changes.

It seems he never changed in his life.

This much-travelled, many-sided and complex man, was he from the outset and to the end a dilettante?

I cannot believe it.

There must be other clues.

Down there, in Wickham Terrace, a man in dress coat, hair cropped, beard trim. But he walks with a stoop. Pulszky never had that. The first time he walked in, despite the quiet air, a certain authority.

His wife. What is it like to be wedded to a beauty? She was – still is, he told me – toast of an entire theatre, the Blonde Wonder of Budapest. The Greatest Actress in Hungary. Well, that says it all. One might almost echo: and who is the Greatest Actress in Australia? Though even in our much-slighted colony that would mean to go out, then, and conquer London. Nellie Melba, I see in last week's newspaper, has London grovelling at her feet.

The theatre is another world. Most curious that Pulszky saw his whole life as part of that profession – and yet he was a man of science, method, precision. It is as if his entire life was an attempt to marry opposites.

His wife, the pretty protégée who overtook him, grew beyond him, held her own court: I can see he was not masterful.

Perhaps she mastered him, and then of course despised him for it. My father was right in recommending that the week of marriage defines the terms, and they must be strictly kept to.

But the stimulus? What I felt, in the end, was a sort of envy. He had come out the other side of a passageway, and even in defeat the knowledge held gave him a look, how shall I say, a look of experience.

In Brisbane I have enough experience. It is all a matter of discipline, and of taking each opportunity, wrenching it to yield its discipline.

How far do we spend our lives in a sort of theatre? This actress wife haunts me, I can see that. But to let theatre create our personality: man is a social being, so it follows theatre composes a large part of action and behaviour.

The gesture of greeting. *Grüss Gott*!

The act of merchant banking, the performance of commerce. Hilarious comedy at the livestock auctions, audience everywhere, the stage small as this consulting room. Deprive us of theatre and the whole spectacle of Government collapses. Print is theatre. Talk is, caresses, argument, anger. The ceremony of identification in morgues.

Very well then; we are bound, actors and actresses. And then, there are critics.

Perhaps in that marriage it was unrestricted experiment?

At what point does the gesture remain real? When does indulgence become a habit? When is the science of discovery merely an old handbill? It is a paradox, and the gods impose some cruel forfeits in paradox.

An Hungarian Art Director in Australia – not so eccentric. I have seen Russian political emigrés, American defectors, there are even Australians who flee to Paraguay – it is not place we flee to, or from, it is ourselves.

Because I *found* myself here in Australia I am too unsympathetic. Perhaps because I could not imagine the theatre of a wife more indulged than myself, and more disciplined, more central in herself and the increase in herself: performance is indeed discipline, as my wife's long practice on scales and arpeggios assures me. In a world given to the imagination, what is reality? Is it a chart of graded letters on a wall? Is it a stethoscope, a black bag and a few carefully modulated gruff inquisitions?

We must cling to something. Here, this newspaper: and what are the news headlines? The Dreyfus case again, more layers of political conspiracy, more lies, more corruption. The most cruel theatre.

Pulszky told me his trial was based on wider political motives: a family too prominent in politics and too dominant in positions of power. Even worse, his father, a national hero, in his old age a ceaseless challenger to the new regime, which sought to crawl

88

backwards towards Austria, selling its hard-won independence – a partial thing at best, like our own dependent Parliaments. He sounds a bluff, brave old man, thumping his stick at the timid young, railing at the clerics and the anti-Semitism that infects the age. Too concerned with standards for the radicals, too radical for the conservatives: a political family, yes, but politicians none of them.

And yet I admire the man. I admired him. The pride he had when talking of his own father. The privilege of being his scape-goat.

I have made my own nest, very comfortable. I like this room. I enjoy good leather and the proper suit, even in tropical summer. Now I am restless in the comfort of it, it is as if I had omitted something in my plans. We do not see what we do not see. We are even more uncomfortable to have it shown to us. This man haunts me now. He is a burr, a thorn that even when extracted leaves its chafe, sometimes for months.

We regard such power as a sort of poison, but that is only because we cannot find the word. He found it and could do nothing. Why, even his last note, which I am entrusted to forward to Budapest, shows how his vision lacked normal efficiency – it is dated the 9th of June: yesterday. He has been dead four days.

If he had those four days, would he have changed? Would I have sought him out again, or even tried persuasion? Case closed.

I was nothing to him. I misinterpreted everything but the documentation of behaviour and performance. I forgot the layers of dimension possible in theatre. I forgot the act of translation.

Emilia Markus receives a letter from Dr Eugen Hirschfeld of Brisbane dated 10 July 1899. It contains news of Károly Pulszky's death. His last letter to her is enclosed, dated 9 June

My own poor Charlie. I cannot live with the knowledge of your death. You throw my anger back into my face and deny me hope of justification. I loved you fearfully, desperately. To admit that is not to deny the desperation, but it helps me explain to myself the galling desperation of those later years. Of course I loved you, you had my body to reassure you, time after time, when the fires had died down. When the fires had died. I cannot live with the knowledge of your death.

We played at elaborate parties. We played games, sometimes with others. Do you remember that dinner we gave in honour of Mari Jaszai? How she rankled at our sweet sincerity and could not think of a function elaborate enough in return. In each lady's place at table you had a marvellous Geisha doll to hold her name. It was a gift. You never confided to me what they cost. We were inheritors of the world then, nothing was too rich. We were stuffed with self-delight like goose liver paste. I was far gone in pregnancy.

I wept uncontrollably that night, later. I recall the weeping but not the cause. You were so tender, so understanding, so puzzled. I cannot live with the knowledge of your death.

I told you, then, I had never loved you, I had never loved anybody. I had never loved your body.

I lied.

Mari Jaszai   Mari Jaszai   Mari Jaszai   You joked me out of it, you said I would grow like her if I tried the rôle of Tragic Matriarch. You turned my anger into a game of titters against Mari. She will never know.

I still lie to myself. I still suffer. I cannot envisage your death.

You knew me better than any other person in my life. You moulded me into your life, you made me your ideal. I half believed the goddess you knelt to, you knew it was a rôle that might convince the world.

Ah Charlie, we have no more English lessons, no instruction programmes to look to now, no arguments. You will not grow impatient at my own impatience any more. I cannot believe anything. I cannot live with the knowledge of your death.

'What is your life for?' I once demanded of you. You smiled, and then turned serious. That was only nights before the newspapers ripped you apart.

I will never understand my anger then, nor why, in the end, when it was all done, when the outrage was over and you were released, that anger turned on you. You had been absolved of charges. You knew me too well. I did not have to say a syllable.

Once, even our arguments were a way of sharing delight and challenge. Others were sometimes alarmed, but we were invulnerable.

I would not follow you, but that is not to say I lost you, or lost thought of you, in far Australia. My poor, poor Charlie. I could kick you, pinch you, tweak you, to wake you from that noble withdrawal. Anything, to forestall knowledge of your death.

And you haunt me. You lay snares for me, still. Why, as the good Doctor writes, if you died on the 5th of June, why did you date this letter the 9th? Why, Charlie, why?

Why deceive me? How could I believe in the truth of that good Doctor's letter claiming you died four days before, and by your own hand? Were you wanting to cushion me, again, from your impulsiveness? Did you think I could not bear the truth? To discover a soft core of dishonesty even in this is to commit the cruellest thing, as if even your final act were not offered seriously, as if you might shuffle the consequences, yet again, so I could not notice, so I 'would not be hurt'.

Your letter has a tone of complaint. You were never open in anything. How can I believe your profession of guilt, or your mistakes? Yes, you strove always to make others happy. As if they could not endure the truth. I cannot live with the knowledge of your death. I cannot live with the uncertainty, still – are you yet lingering there, somewhere in the hot tropics? I do not recognise you.

I am tied to your flesh forever. You throw me back to my anger.
You deny me hope.

When your family cut you out of their lives that was the time
you first stood alone.

Except that I was there. I supported you.

Your family did not cut you out. It was me they excluded. I
knew I had lost you, then.

I cannot live with the knowledge, or your death.

The Nijinskys in Budapest

'On our way to Budapest, my sister met us in Vienna. At last
Vaslav hoped to arrive in a peaceful family circle, but he was
painfully surprised. On our arrival in Budapest, instead of the
loving embrace of a mother, a crowd of reporters, camera-men,
and photographers awaited us. My mother entertained largely,
and we were dragged from one reception to the other, stared at
like strange animals from the jungle, and questioned. I knew
Vaslav was disappointed, but he never said anything, and politely
went wherever my mother wished us to go . . .

'We arrived in Budapest on a hot summer day – the 23rd July
1914. A dreadful storm broke out – almost a hurricane – that
broke all the windows at my mother's villa, and the big bell of
the St Stephan Basilica fell. "Some misfortune is going to happen", one of my mother's peasant maids declared. Next day I saw
in the papers that an ultimatum had been sent to Serbia . . .

'In half an hour we stood before the chief of the detective
bureau. In fluent French he said: "Mr and Mrs Nijinsky, in the
name of the military authorities I am obliged to arrest you and
your daughter Kyra as enemy subjects. All three of you have to
remain wherever you will be allotted on our territory until the
termination of hostilities, as prisoners of war." . . . We were told
that we were to stay at my mother's house, confined until further
orders. We must report every week to the police and avoid passing
barracks, fortifications or any building of a military nature. All
correspondence must cease, of course. We were supposed to pay
all expenses . . .

'One day we were again summoned to the police for some kind of registration. A young bureaucrat, feeling extremely important in his new uniform, questioned us. When I gave him my maiden name, he looked up. "What! Romola de Pulszky, the grand-daughter of the great Francis de Pulszky, the first founder of Hungarian democracy, the friend of Kossuth? But you are Hungarian."

' "No," I answered, "I am the grand-daughter of Francis de Pulszky, but I am the wife of Nijinsky and a Russian now."

' "You should divorce," he said.

' "I thought you were here to fill in the slips for the prisoners, not to give advice." And I turned my back on him.

'Next day the papers were full of the incident. They called me a "traitor" ... So intrigues began to make me divorce Vaslav, naturally without success, but the constant nagging was painful.

'I now knew not only how unwelcome Vaslav was in my mother's house, but that he was despised, and he, with his fine instincts, began to feel it too. We were not allowed to leave the house and more and more he withdrew from everybody into Kyra's room. But soon my mother penetrated even there, and began to give orders concerning the upbringing of the child ... The servants, seeing my mother's attitude, refused to serve us. Soon we had to do most of the things ourselves, but this we did not mind. We received our food very irregularly, sometimes lunch at four or five in the afternoon, and I saw that Vaslav felt faint ...

'For many months I watched him designing and counting, drawing with infinite care; sometimes very late at night, I awoke from my sleep and Vaslav was still bowed over his writing-desk. My mother complained he used too much electricity.

'I became interested in his work, which seemed like geometry, like mathematics, and which was neither. Vaslav was pleased by my suddenly manifested interest, and explained to me that he was attempting to find a system through which dances and all human movements could be written down ... "Music can be noted; so can words; but unfortunately dancing cannot. And so the most precious compositions get lost and are forgotten ..."

'... My mother became more irritable with Vaslav, and for everything that went wrong in or round the house, he was blamed, first secretly, then openly. The automatic boiler of the hot-water system broke. "Mr Nijinsky must have spoiled it," said the valet.

My mother forbade him to take a bath or use hot water . . . And then one day my mother's pet cat disappeared. It was a fat, old, ordinary cat . . . She flew into a rage. "It is Vaslav; he must have killed the cat." Vaslav's eyes closed; his face was immobile. He looked very much like a Tibetan lama. Everybody was in an uproar; they all searched for the cat. "There she is, darling Mima," said the valet, and pointed to a linden tree, in which the cat blissfully browsed, and my cousin's dog was lying in wait at the bottom of the tree watching her.

'But this did not make any difference to my mother. She turned to Vaslav, convulsed with rage, and screamed: "You hateful man, you damned Russian you! You are the one who did it. I wish you were out of my house for ever, you silly acrobat, you circus dancer!" . . .

'What to do? I did a bold thing. I asked Vaslav to let me go to Vienna . . . He was rather anxious on account of the risk I was taking. Should I be discovered, they would arrest and punish me. But I was born a Hungarian. It was my native country and language . . . Vaslav could spend the day at my Aunt Poly's, who did not like my mother and had ceased all relationship with her at the death of my father years ago. So at home they would not notice that I was away . . . I carried out my plan successfully . . . I had to see my godfather, His Excellency Thallocy, who at that time was one of the five members of the War Council residing at the War Office . . .

'He pulled a serious, strict face, but as soon as we were left alone he said, "You Russian subject, I am going to arrest you and send you to gaol. The idea of penetrating to the War Office, when our respective troops are fighting at Przemysl!" Then he kissed me and patted me on my shoulders and said, "In spite of it all, I like your bravery and your loyalty to your husband. That is how it should be; that is the way Hungarian women have been through the ages. No, to send you to concentration camp is impossible . . . I will see what I can do. Of course, I know your mother; she is a great woman, lovely; I was very much in love with her in my youth. A very, very great actress, but as a mother-in-law – brrrr! I can just imagine. But, you stupid child, can't you understand? Don't you know human psychology? Your mother, the great artist, was chained to Hungary all her life. Her success

94

never passed the frontiers, because she played in Hungarian. Your husband's art is universal." . . .

'Next morning, while I was still in bed, a detective came to fetch us. We reported to the police. Vaslav and I were immediately separated at the entrance, led into different rooms, and questioned. For hours I was put under cross-examination; so was Vaslav. I could not make out at what they were driving. The chief told me. "I understand that for months your husband was working on some kind of a plan. It is a military one. Do you know it? It must be some code. Our attention was called to it by patriotic people."

' "Ridiculous! My husband is working on the system of notation of the human movements. Ever since the time of Louis XIV dancers have been searching for it. It is true that he spends the greater part of his day, till late in the night, on this work. But it has no more to do with war or military schemes than the canals of Mars." . . .

'Experts of music and mathematics were called in, and Vaslav explained to them his system. It took several days of investigations, and then those men congratulated him on his epoch-making creation. The next time we reported, I insisted on knowing from our chief who had denounced us.

' "I cannot say; it is an official secret. But it was really a ridiculous thing to do. It also put us in a rather awkward position, but we had to investigate the matter once it was brought to our notice. Of course, we were told Nijinsky was working on a military plan."

' "But who – who could have insinuated anything of the sort?"

' "Well, well, over-anxious, blinded persons, who are perhaps rather nervous about their own position. Family misunderstandings often cause remarkable events."

'I understood he referred to my parents. "Did it come from home? Please, please say."

'He bowed his head and said, "Don't ask me, but I wish you could be sent to some other place of internment".'

(from *Nijinsky*, Romola Nijinsky-Pulszky)

'In the Emilia Markus household, talent, that is, real talent, was regarded as a divine favour that gave one the right to enjoy many other favours: luxury and comfort of lifestyle, high-society connections, vanity, selfishness and caprice. Romola encountered the other side of the coin when she brought an unwanted son-in-law to her mother's house. And she grew to hate her mother with all the force of her pampered and obstinate nature. However, the way of life to which she had been accustomed since childhood remained her criterion. She was guided by it and wished to "reshape" her husband accordingly.

'But Nijinsky, who felt he had been a prisoner all his life, did not realise that such imprisonment was more worthy. He did not realise that, in separating him from Diaghilev, Romola was separating him from genuine art, from free experimentation, from trial and error.'

(from *Nijinsky*, Vera Krasovskaya)

'And, while lying there in the scented pasture, we spoke of many things. I told Vaslav about my parents' unhappy marriage, and blamed my mother, but he stopped me. "Don't be hard. You do not know the circumstances that made her act the way she did. We should never condemn anybody, nor have we the right to judge".'

(from *Nijinsky*, Romola Nijinsky-Pulszky)

1896. February 5th. Budapest

Report in the newspaper the *Budapesti Hirlap*

Today the Capital, even the whole Country, is talking about the Pulszky case. Is he really insane? Well, insane or not, he was taken to the asylum this morning. Whatever the truth, according to a semi-official government report, he has escaped into illness after three ministerial reminders and an Inquiry. He could not, or would not, account for the large amount of money entrusted to him, and members of the investigating team found a completely apathetic man, suffering from fits. His friends are saying that the

96

amount of travel, all work and no rest, would affect anybody. If this were true, every commercial traveller would go mad.

Secondly, he often travelled with his wife or others, in absolute luxury. In Venice he hired two gondolas and his feverish buying allowed him time to entertain the actress Madame Duse to night music by lanterns. His lifestyle at home, with countless carriages, expensive ladies from the music-hall, notorious night revels, seems more that of a Nabob than a madman.

The Government, though not wanting to implicate Pulszky too much, must put all the blame on him to save itself from looking negligent.

After not being able to account for 7,000 florins he was given 204,000 more. He was allowed to spend on the worthless Piombo 'painting' (well known by Italian experts not to be Rafael's work for more than twenty years), a maximum of 115,000 florins. After he bought it through the Countess Chevigné, he sent a telegram saying he must pay her 135,000 francs. The Countess paid 131,000 francs for it.

The investigators found a large number of unopened letters on Pulszky's desk from art dealers abroad, all urging acceptance and payment for goods ordered through them.

We have been told several stories about the latest behaviour of Pulszky. Last summer, Dr Demjanovich was a guest at the property of his parliamentarian friend Gájary. On arrival, he asked the coachman who the other guests were. 'Mr Bakonyi, Mr Deutsch, and that crazy Pulszky.' This was most unusual, coming from a servant. Demjanovich found Pulszky pale, with burning eyes, his voice hoarse. The reason for his hoarseness was that he never stopped talking. His tone was such that he gave the impression of being the only one to understand whatever the subject might be. At dinner, he did not touch his meal, but drank large quantities of strong coffee, and chain-smoked. He shared a bedroom with Deutsch, whom he woke up and told the bewildered man that the night is not for sleeping; there is no need to sleep; and that he had not slept for three months.

On another occasion Pulszky accosted Deutsch in a restaurant and despite the late hour demanded from him, in the name of friendship, to arrange for a horse to wait for him the next morning at a certain country railway station. He was expecting a famous lady archaeologist to arrive there, and decided to escort her carriage on horseback, wearing the Hungarian national gala costume to show off his looks and to impress her.

He got his wish.

Another story: when Weherle was Prime Minister he asked one of Pulszky's friends to explain to him that Pulszky must be more respectful towards his superiors. The man answered: 'I can't tell Károly anything, he is half crazy. The other day while he was visiting me he jumped out the window naked!'

A quote from another newspaper: In the past few weeks the catastrophe has been expected. Pulszky became frighteningly excited about small matters at work. But no wonder; his travelling partners all became ill, after that much travelling. He had no rest in the past two years, spent most of his time in trains. When he was at home, he suddenly developed a passion for horse riding, and started to wear his officer's uniform (to which he was not entitled at that time). He told his friends that he intended to become the best equestrian on the continent. This eccentric behaviour changed a few weeks ago to utter apathy. His adored younger daughter became seriously ill with scarlet fever, and he did not once visit her. He was incapable of doing anything. In the meantime a large consignment of old books arrived: 50,000 cartons and bill for 15,000 florins. Nobody knows anything about this, and Pulszky is unable to give an explanation.

Part IV: Son and Father

'No outward change ...'

Károly Pulszky remembers

'One autumn night in 1821 a gentleman came in great haste to my father, softly spoke a few words to him, upon which father – against his usual custom as he never went out at night – fetched his hat and left the house. My mother took us children next door to the Heman's, whose children we often played with; here, we noisily entertained ourselves all evening and to our astonishment stayed overnight and returned home only at noon the next day. No outward change was visible on father or mother, and routine in the home was in no way disturbed, although the news which surprised them yesterday was that my brother Laci shot himself at the Cemetery ... Even later, my father never mentioned the loss of his son.'

(from My Life and Times, Ferenc Pulszky)

I seem to be much taken with recollecting things. Perhaps it is a way to order. Perhaps it is a way out of order. It is, I discover, so simple and efficient to prescribe. I have been taught. To my daughters more than half the world away it is an art of instruction that comes so quickly the letter is all done before I say the things I want to say. I cannot say them. I envied my mother's deft hand with anecdote and recall, it was always as if she were the traveller and the world a witty place to observe.

I smart to know how she would write of this awkward village, Brisbane. I write nothing. I observe nothing. I have failed my resources, my mother would not forgive.

And yet, three years ago, how eagerly I might have come as a visitor, amused at their new Art Gallery with its shy copies and dull English Academicians, curious about museum artefacts and the scratchings of more ancient cultures. I might – who knows – have begun their new Art Gallery.

I amuse myself by this. To begin from nothing, nowhere, would be beyond my resources, even those of my prime. So much was given me at birth, I never had to work without the finest tools, or the most scrupulous concerns. I might have gone my entire life

101

without a fine appreciation of the weakness in aesthetic theory, faced with such beginnings as these. My life was born out of a thousand years of endings, more beginnings, endless rebirth. I inherited my parents' cultures and worked hard upon my birthright. I insist my children must do the same. It is all they might, in the end, cling to, and is gold currency.

People here bewail how quickly so many inherited or imported values are lost, even to their first-born. They say education is the first to suffer, then culture. Their children play in unkempt ground and make it their own. Some call it regression, but maybe it is a necessary initiation or a stage of rebirth. Some grow impatient at foreign imposition and stay out in the sun. In this climate, it is hard to remain inside, where the rooms are so dull and the people timid. A culture is not brought with counterpanes and antimacassars though these indeed may be the tokens of a certain balance achieved. To start again, and to learn to discard, acquire, or transfigure: so many reasons for timidity, none of them convincing.

The local opera-house tonight plays *The Convict's Escape* and *The Outcast's Dream*. In Budapest, it will be Wagner, Mozart, or the new Mascagni. Or else Erkel or Cornelius.

We have endured a thousand years. So. How do I apply my resources of a thousand years? Luxurious Budapest, your resources all became indulgences and self-indulgences, now I must look at them from this glassy light, the first light in the world. How does one start again? Trial and error, free experimentation? It is not possible; too many things have been brought with our very genes, language itself invents too many old knots to bind us back beyond centuries to an identity we may never disavow, only tug against, sullenly. With me. With all of them here.

My father warned constantly of our complacency in Budapest, and the price we would pay. He echoed Kossuth's most famous prophecy, that the Compromise we made with Austria destroyed the only hope of an independent eastern Europe.

It is rather the way these colonials make their compromise, clinging to an inflated power base in London that is not their own. Do they realise how scornful England is of their obsequious dependency? Aquincum was an outpost of Rome, but had learned the Roman values of proper tribute, and improper. Independence is the hardest thing of all yet it is the only basis for

102

growth. Even Aquincum died, cut from its source. My father was right to bully me with concepts of independence and self-sufficiency.

I thought I understood what that meant.

My exile is a way of asking myself what things I bring with me out of a holocaust. Kossuth saw Europe consumed in an eventual holocaust, if his Danubian policies were disregarded. My father swore he was right. Our century promised so many revolutions, but has produced merely colonies. And the power to seduce the colonies seemingly forever.

My father.

What things do I bring alone? A head full of references and footnotes. A family that I know I have lost. A sense of myself that is seen by every storekeeper and innkeeper in this town as a failed man's way of selling insurance. I have no Life in me.

The credibility of the new life here is not mine, but it is undoubted, in its own way. It is based on unbelief. And then upon a belief in almost anything.

I am reminded of my father's story of the Praying Indians. They tempered their unbelief by a new belief in almost anything. The willingness of the new convert is awesome. These people here pretend a disaffection and a hardy lack of affectation but they are the most attracted by glass beads and mirrors.

Romola, my Tessa, I would have said to you: persevere, be persistent, learn all you can for as long as you can; it is your only guard against life's dangers, and it is all there is. And yet I betray my words unremittingly. Who would have thought one's belief in one's own self could die so efficiently? Who would believe that place could be so insubstantial? It is all we are brought out of, all we are given to.

The Praying Indians

'Originally the conflicts between the Indians and English were the natural consequences of the collision between hunter and agriculturalist. But, after the war had begun and blood had been spilt for a whole century, it was no longer of any avail for the red man to exchange the rifle for the plough, and the moveable wigwam for a fixed settlement. Moravian missionaries had carried the gospel among the Delawares; they had overcome their distrust; they had escaped the plots of the savages against their lives; they had converted some leading Indians; and their pure and truly Christian life of kindness and resolution had a deep influence on the Wyandots in the neighbourhood. The converts increased daily; they settled on the Muskingum, in three communities; distinguished by their meekness, industry, and religiousness. They had accepted the gospel by conviction, and observed, therefore, its injunctions with more devoutness than the whites, as all primitive nations do with the tenets of a religion new to them.

'They were hospitable towards every stranger, whether white or red; and when the revolutionary war began in 1775, they had not learnt to make any distinction between English and American, or the allies of each of them. They entertained every party which crossed the settlement with the same kindness, and furnished supplies to them. Friends of peace, and believing war a sin against God, they did all they could to prevail on the Ohio Indians to live in peace; and when they knew of any hostile parties intending an attack on the settlements, they sent runners, and gave them a timely warning. But in times of war the peaceful become an offence to both the belligerents. The "praying Indians" as they were called, were suspected by both the English and Americans . . .

'The English determined at last to remove them from the American boundary, and in 1781, the Iroquois, who acted as lords paramount of the West, were asked at a council to have the "praying Indians" carried away. The subject was considered by the six nations at Niagara, but they declined to do it themselves; they therefore sent a message to the Ottowas and Ojibbeways, with the words: "We herewith make you a present of the Christian Indians, to make soup of". Both the tribes declined the treat; they returned for answer: "We have no cause for doing this" . . .

'The English commander, after having punished them severely, at last suffered some of their number to return in February, 1782; others remained under English "protection".

'The Americans, seeing that the English had released some of the Christian Indians, took it for an evidence of their treachery

104

and secret understanding with the enemy, and, as several families were killed during winter along the Ohio, by the savage Delawares, those massacres were imputed to the "praying Indians".

'Colonel Williamson, therefore, collected an irregular force of about one hundred men, and made a rapid march ...

'As the hostile force appeared, the Christian Indians ran to their village. There they were told that they were to be removed to Pittsburg, for protection during the war, and were directed to enter two houses, the males in one, the females in the other. The inhabitants of the neighbouring village, Salem, were also decoyed there; after which they were bound, and well guarded. The Commander of the party held in the evening a council, to determine how the "Moravian Indians" should be disposed of; he put the question, whether they should be taken prisoners to Pittsburg, or put to death.

'Of some ninety men present, only seventeen voted for mercy; it was therefore announced to the Indians that they had to prepare for death. The poor victims spent the night in prayers and in singing hymns; in the morning they were murdered in cold blood, by guns, tomahawks, and hatchets, in number 40 men, 22 women and 32 children. The buildings were then set on fire, and the bodies partially consumed.'

(from *White, Red, Black*, Francis and Theresa Pulszky)

The Moravian Indians was a story I always demanded of my father, in those early years when I knew him. He was so much away. After my mother's death, in his house we were separated by our similarities. He thought me possessive of his art treasures, and I was. From his collections of ivories, statues and fine tapestries I stole his own acquisitiveness from him.

As an older student I dressed with my friends in the genuine crowns and cummerbunds and robes of ancient princes, in the museum where my father was Director. My playthings were very valuable and part of the National Treasure. He was amused, and indulged me. We did no harm.

Later, I did not understand the anger of others, hearing of our larks. I thought them merely jealous of my privilege. I took so many things for granted.

Latterly it is a shock for me to realise the Moravian Indians are fellows in credulity with me. I believed everything. 'Of some

105

ninety men present, only seventeen voted for mercy.' In my case it was a smaller number. There is some law of proportion that guides these statistics. My father thought to give me security, position, privilege. If even the humble of this earth are consumed by blood-lust and a fear that lashes like a serpent at them, the privileged walk through a crowded city of the envious and the dispossessed. There is not one person who walks harmlessly and without the murderous envy of another. The Moravian Indians were privileged in one simple thing: belief.

I do not blame them, now, for this. Knowledge is the best defence. Self-knowledge is a bottomless pool, but the envy of others is purged from it. My father was so confident he had given me everything. When, in old age, he remarried, he could not understand how hateful we were. But his battle scars were like old armour. He was of the warlike tribes. He did not need what we refused to give him.

'No outward change was visible on father or mother, and routine in the home was in no way disturbed ... even later, my father never mentioned the loss of his son ...'

I remember when I first saw Budapest. I was twelve, my mother just returned from exile in London, my first home. The wooded slopes of the Buda mountains with the broad band of the Danube declared me their hostage, instantly. Even the sandy dust of the Rákos and the flat plains beyond Pest in those years had a wildness that excited me.

Brisbane, flat to the sea with its river pushing back the hills has strange echoes and an aftertaste. What foretaste might it offer? Some things are impossible. Budapest those first years was small, provincial, palace and walls, cathedral, fragments – in my own lifetime it became a plan brought to acclaim. The boulevards and trees of Pest, the dream of order realised yet retaining an early wildness. On Margaret Island I would wander all summer, lost in pure forest reveries. Even now I would spend hours there. I still see the candle flowers of horse-chestnut.

Exile strips the trees in this wilderness, and knots them with knobbled growths, warts, diseases ... on Margaret Island I fought a duel once with an enemy of my father.

My father is dead and my enemies prosper, they are even at

this moment thwacking their knives on the table, they sniff and lip for their latest raw meat which was my whole life in art. Géza Polonyi with his talk of 'corruption' and János Felenyalc with my 'mad money sacrifice from the National Fortune to purchase beautiful faces and lips by Rafael'; they should crawl in the dust to approach what I brought them. I found them a pure orchard with fountain and wall. Someone – my daughters perhaps – will enter there to be nourished. Someone will begin to understand what I created in the National Gallery out of a tangle of princes' enthusiasms and a few miscellaneous donations. Let them bay and yelp at the gate. In their rich houses they are exiles.

I am shut out of that orchard.

Várády also, returning again and again to the smell of my ripped entrails, slavering, ripping, on fire to reach for the heart-fire: enmity refines him. He will be locked out forever. He will thirst till his tongue bloats.

He lives it up now.

I spit my full curse on him. I curse Polonyi. I curse all of them, in that Party, in that Parliament, in Budapest. May the Hordes return on them, may their children be twisted and their grand-children grind stone against steel without freedom, may the lovely streets fester and shatter, let it return to its desert and sand and may Buda with all its hill terraces find pure bile in its fountains and fresh blood in its mineral springs. May the locusts descend. May there be exile and homelessness, may it be unending.

Two months and it is unending. So much for curses. This Brisbane is a rough town without fingerprints and with no direction. Nothing is planned, there are no boulevards, no gardens, no forest walks. Women jump over mud, nothing is paved, the tallest buildings jostle and contradict each other. It has a remorseless vigour born of exile and cupidity. It will prosper from rootlessness. They say it was drowned six years back. They have filled in those marshes for subdivisions – that sort of prosperity. In my lifetime I saw a true city rise from sand wastes. Perhaps loss is inevitable. Let all my enemies dwell in this exile.

I will never return to unreal Budapest or its reality. I could not believe myself so entirely hated. Forgive me, father, I am glad you did not wait longer. It was my name they were pack-dogs for. It was your blood in my prison, my exile is, I acknowledge, half yours. Your blessing has struck me down, your humiliation destroyed me. Forgive me, father, forgive my curses. I must learn to hate entirely.

Another June morning. And another. Here it slaps down sunlight like splinters, nothing hazy or soft. On the 6th of June three years ago I stepped out of my Gallery dishonoured. My crime? Acquisition of 151 paintings, 49 frescoes, 114 sculptures, 29 works on paper and 602 engravings. My crime? To see and acquire for Hungary works of such finesse that the national purpose in millennium year would be accomplished: more, I created that National Gallery.

My crime? To be a Pulszky, to know what I saw, and to rush headstrong towards excellence.

For this I was charged with embezzlement, buying fakes, buying extravagantly. More: incompetence, immorality, bad judgment. Three months I was held, after arrest, before those charges were withdrawn. Nothing else was withdrawn. Even my wife sniffed for the guilt-smell behind her loyal performance of support and belief in me. Only a married man can know to perfection the loss of his credibility. All learning comes to artifice. Perhaps no one is guilty, perhaps everyone is. I plead guilty to the charge of art. To the charge of seeing with a fine drunkenness the forgeries by Piero di Cosimo of a Christ Byzantine on the Cross, not naked. To the charge of revealing Ghiberti (or his followers) who saw the Virgin and Child with sadness and compassion; of Jacobo della Quercia describing the Holy Pair as spider and host; of Michelozzo Michelozzi with them firm in soft radiance – all forgeries in the way art is, all fleeting, all profound.

Stillness is forgery in this knife-edge world. Three months without trial and in custody. Numbness stopped in the room with me. Feeling withdraws from us; hearing, touching, consciousness. No one could goad me, those months. Nothing.

Loss, though, takes away more than feeling. Another June morning, it might be called 'beautiful'. It is called loss loss and the return of loss bites into me, into the no-feeling where flesh and sensation should be. On the 6th of June I will be lost again, and for another year, eternally, in this far country in this splintering sunshine. To many things I am guilty. I taught myself to see and to believe in the vision I traded upon. I was a dutiful son. I was no son at all. I envied the coarse honesty of my father, and

108

the finesse of his younger life. I mocked him slyly. So it falls. I could be anyone but am not. To the end I am a Pulszky whatever that means.

Only one last regret: this withdrawal of feeling, this loss of appetite, this smell, this husk, this prison limiting me. If I could still feel rage, fire, murder ... I take my meals with absence, as if I sneered at everything. I taste the dryness and I must make it my feast.

'... No outward change was visible on father or mother, and routine in the home was in no way disturbed ... even later, my father never mentioned the loss of his son ...'

Part V: The Old Law

Károly Pulszky talks to the sunlight

'Water and mud have dried in the pond.
My Lord, my dear God, give us a good rain.
The poor beasts hunch . . . there is nothing to graze upon.
These times grow sorrow, these times grow ruin;
I confess I am tired . . .'
                                    All our folksongs weep.
'My sad heart will never have rest.' We all
have hurried the old words. Nothing to keep
pure in the sunlight. Nothing to spoil,
out in the open. Nothing to keep still.

I am the nothing that even this sunlight caressed.
Sunlight moves into the nothing. It will lie down
anywhere. My entire body is a feast.
Sunlight scoops as if it had a tongue.
Cattle tongue pushes in. My salt is gone.

Sunlight always licks with a hard edge.
It invents appetite. I am dry grass.
It has an appetite for salt sedge.
Grass trampled to nothing. It feasts on loss.
Water, mud, stalks in the sun, nothing less.

The Comtesse de Chevigné and her lady companion take breakfast at the Grand Hotel Duomo

— Amalie, do you think that some sharp-toothed little rodent has been nibbling at the heart of dear little Charlie Pulszky – no, pull the sash further, there's a dear – did you notice his agitation last night? It's really too bad. Do you think, perhaps, that his famous and glorious marriage might have turned into something of a cage?

— They say a caged rat has been known to tear at its own body in a sort of desperation ...

— Can that be true? Yes, I am sure you are right in these things, you are so thorough. Our dear Charlie was certainly not himself, truly. I've never seen him so miserably excited, and all over this auction today. You'd think with his experience he'd be on top of it all. No. Some little rat is in there gnawing at the marrow. My God, it's not *me*, d'ye think?

— Madame la Comtesse, it's not for me to say ...

— Amalie, don't be a guineafowl! But do you think that Charlie Pulszky has really taken a crush on me? D'ye know, it's not till this moment that it has even occurred to me. Well, flattering. But he must be out of his cataloguing mind, all the same, a man in his position, and I am sure without a franc of his own. Eh bien, it's always the case.

— He has been most singular, these two days ...

— Singular? Plural, my dear, multiple, many, a host – why, Charlie has turned into a veritable chameleon, he acts out more parts than his singular wife. Hah. Well, dear man, I am fond of him really. But, oh lordy, to be an object of passion again. Well, this I know and he does too, it can't be my money! Well, what d'ye say? Has that guineafowl taken your tongue now?

— I was thinking, madame, of that little tête-à-tête you had together over supper, about the Scarpa auction today ...

— No. I say no. Amalie, you will not say a thing. I will not be stopped from my little fun. I think I would make an absurdly fine

114

bidder at auctions. Especially if the cash is not my own. And more especially if it is to do a personal favour to a very dear friend like Charlie Pulszky. And most, indeed most especially if it is not his money either, but that of those parliamentary Hungarians. I did tell you about the time I last stayed with my husband's dreadful family at Schönbrunn – if only I had your companionship that visit, oh it would have prevented indescribable ennui – and thinking his deaf old aunt the Princess was indeed a deaf old aunt I could not prevent myself from groaning aloud at the latest long tedious supper we were plunging into. I murmured 'oh the boredom of it!' in what was, for me, a positively dulcet contralto. And the old crow turned round like a marionette, quick as a flash, and patted my lap with her fan. 'Never mind, my dear, it will pass', she solicited. Quelle honte! What a moment! I held my counsel after that, I assure you. Well. These Austrians, these Austro-Hungarians! Where was I at?

— Madame, it seems we are at the auction. Or nearly at.

— Exactly. Well, I will go. I will do Charlie's bidding, at least in this. No no, you must not stop me. Perhaps I will not stop myself! Shall I mortgage his gallery for a million? Where shall I stop? I know once I have the horse by the reins nothing will stop me. 'Get me the Piombo portrait', he said, 'get it by any means possible, but get it', he said.

— And you promptly reminded him of the commission fee . . .

— I did not! I thought I handled that with some little finesse, Amalie you monstrous guineafowl, now do not contradict me.

— Shall I remind you of your precise words, Madame . . .

— You daren't! Really, what did I say? I committed no bêtise.

— Monsieur Pulszky himself suggested it.

— Naturally.

— He also suggested there were limits.

— As well he might. Why do I not remember these details?

— It was late in the evening, and you had been engaged in a most vehement discussion . . .

— Yes of course. It was on tactics. Most interesting. That man is a walking encyclopaedia. But last night by the end I felt the encyclopaedia's pages were whistling around me, the tomes out of order, the bookcase itself quite unstable, in danger of toppling. Well, I do not wish to be underneath when that happens. You recall Monsieur Alkan? I think I am too young, really, to be crushed by the burden of books. Taken singly, they are wonderfully soporific. By the caseful, they're damned dangerous.

— One moment, Madame, that was somebody knocking . . .

— Charlie! My god, Charlie, talk of the devil. Why, what's got into you, you're as white as the Matterhorn!

— Madame la Comtesse. Mademoiselle. I'm too early? No. I will call back later. But the auction is about to happen . . .

— Charlie, oh for heaven's sake stop the man, Amalie. Charlie, do not skittle away like that. You upset me. Yes, you do. Now, be a dear boy and skit over here. Coffee? Tea? Why, he's shaking, Amalie. Charlie, what is the matter?

— I am sorry. I did not sleep last night. But I never do. This auction really does have me in its clutches, most unusual. Most unusual for me, I assure you. It is that Piombo.

— Not a word. You talked Piombo Piombo at me all last night till it rattled my brains and only a good cigar settled them. Well, it did. Oh dear boy, don't be so offended; you really are in a state. Strap him down, Amalie, force him to have just one coffee. There, now just sit a moment, Charlie, you pace like a lion.

— My apologies.

— Fiddlesticks, don't get formal with me. At least, not just now, when we are so deeply together in this scandalous assignation. Oh Charlie, just a smile? There. Charlie, the pacing lion – does that flatter you? It's exactly how you look. Though Amalie and I were before addressing ourselves to the question of whether there was something more insidious attacking you, I think we thought of a rat at your gizzard . . .

— The rat is a colony of rats, I feel. I am sorry if it has become visible. I had a dream last night, but not rats. I had become the white stag of Magor; there were hunters . . .

— That's more like! Dear dear Charlie, but of course, how appropriate. The white stag of Magor. It is yourself, nothing surer. However did we think puny vermin-like rats in the same breath as our Charlie? I like the image. The white stag. But do not tell me all your dream, you must not pass on secrets.

— Just one secret. About the Piombo, why I must have it . . .

— I knew. Amalie, I just knew there was something more to that portrait than the cost of it.

— I would have told you last night. I think I intended to. Last night was important to me. Madame. You do realise that – that

116

importance? But I resolved not to burden you with my last secret, the secret purpose I have in acquiring the Piombo. You will forgive me. It is perhaps rather silly, if you view the matter coldly. But I am unable to view the matter coldly at all ...

— You, Charlie? Dear man, am I to be flattered by all this? Or am I to be indulgent?

— The Piombo is a portrait of myself. It is me, that young man, painted three hundred years back.

— Really? Oh really Charlie, now you have taken the edge off things for me. I thought your confession might be somewhat more – fanciful?

— I am sorry if this seems impertinent. It is a secret I have been tossing with, all last night. There is nobody but yourself I dare tell it to. Since you agreed to stand in for me at the bidding, I have been wrestling in my mind whether I should confess to you the real meaning of the portrait for me. You do see, you have become an important figure in my secret obsessions.

— Obsessions indeed. Ah well. Really Charlie, we all have moments of obsession – of infatuation. You with a portrait. Me, with the novelty of acting at your bidding, yes, with acting as your agent. You like that? Of course you do, you are delighted at the indescribable effrontery of persuading me to accept a commission for work done on your behalf. Well, why not, why not indeed? We will keep our bargain.

— Dear Comtesse, don't be angry, I only want to share the particular urgency I feel about that work. I want you to understand ...

— Of course I understand. You see yourself in the daub. Well, why not?

— Tell the truth, Madame, I also had been struck, yesterday, when Monsieur Pulszky showed us the work, with the similarity ...

— Amalie! Little guineafowl, and you did not tell me!

— Lying awake last night, tossing, it became imperative to me that I must tell you. It is almost as if I must tell you, in order to stave off a sense of vertigo, of impending calamity.

— You cannot afford the budget? Aha, Charlie! Now I have it: you are suddenly alarmed, you think I will lead the bids too high for your purse – or for your Hungarian exchequer!

— No. no. We discussed all that, I do not ...

117

— No? Be careful, Charlie. Amalie, look how he blanches. I think I will . . . no, I think I will not. Come over closer, Charlie. Tell me your real purpose in this auction.

— To see myself in that portrait is to become alarmed, Madame, at some deep disquiet within myself. To discover that I have been defined, even before I was born: it is both a fascination and a sort of prophecy. No, not a prophecy. That portrait is just on the edge of moving away from me, moving back into some past I have never known and some future that could not have been foretold. Its very stillness is not stillness at all, but a means of emphasising the vortex.

— Vortex? You keep speaking of some vortex?

— The Piombo portrait, with its immobility, it has been waiting for me through all these centuries. But only for the person I recognise in it at this very moment. Ten years ago, I would never have dreamed to see my self in its face, and ten years hence, I will not be caught with that precision. Do you see? We only recognise the vortex that drags us madly in if we encounter the pressure of stillness. If we grasp the rock of timelessness. Then have it torn from our grasp.

— So I must buy you that rock, that portrait? Well, dear Charlie, I think you play decidedly self-indulgent games. What will you do with it? Hang it above your desk? Replace your mirror?

— My sense of a vortex is real. Yes, I will be truthful with you. I will use it as a charm. The vortex we live through is partly of our own making. I will look on the Piombo, and I will achieve a measure of calm.

— You sound as if you were, not in a vortex as you call it, but in a cage. What did you say, Amalie, earlier? A rat, caged, has been known to feast on itself . . .

— Be careful. Some things we can never own.

— Amalie, do you think I should go on with this thing? I think Charlie might be indeed using me. Is that fair of him?

— . . .

— Come on then. Let us see how far he is prepared to pay.

From records of the Hungarian National Parliament, Parliamentary Session No. 551

KÁROLY VÁRÁDY: Honourable members! (Hear, hear!) I take the liberty to demand an explanation regarding the accounts of the National Art Gallery. Some articles appeared in yesterday's newspapers with the conclusion that the Director of the National Art Gallery did not account for the spending of large amounts of money. My question is based on the report of the *Pesti Naplo* [Pest Diary] which I will read to you:

'In the Parliament and in the political clubs it has been mentioned for weeks that the Director of the National Art Gallery has not yet rendered an account of the large amounts given to him by the Government for the purpose of purchasing works of art for the Gallery.'

In a further passage of the paper:

'Hundreds of thousands went through Károly Pulszky's hands, of which, as we know, no official accounting exists. The facts should be discovered by a strict investigation. The paintings bought by Pulszky should also be examined by international experts, so that any suspicions that the country's money was wasted on worthless objects could be eliminated.'

Hon. Members! These two paragraphs make it my duty to put the question to the Minister. I ask the Minister: did the Director of the National Gallery account for the several hundred thousand florins which were placed at his disposal by the Government for the purpose of purchases to establish the National Gallery of Fine Arts?

GZULA WLASSICS (Minister for Education & Religious Affairs): Hon. Members! I am very pleased that my Hon. Colleague has brought up this question.

(From the far Left: You are pleased?)

119

GZULA WLASSICS: It is not the fact of the matter that is so pleasing but the fact that the Minister is given the opportunity to answer straight away; and as we are speaking about the great art treasures of the Nation, I am permitted to give the frankest explanation and reassurance. (Hear, hear!) I am going to give you the facts from the relevant files, to show you how things stand against those newspaper reports. The Director of the National Art Gallery informed the then Minister of Cultural Affairs Count Czaky, on 28.11.1893, that the Italian market situation was very advantageous; gave a detailed explanation why this was so, then told him that during his recent trip he preselected old paintings and sculptures to the value of 167,560 florins, and he asked for an extraordinary Loan, so that these works could be purchased for the future Museum ... At the request of Count Czaky the Prime Minister and Finance Minister of that time put 167,560 florins at the disposal of the Ministry of Culture. Pulszky submitted his report on the purchases on 17.12.1894, and this revealed that he made purchases for 167,000 florins, but as the market for buying was very favourable in Italy, he felt one should take advantage of this situation. So, in view of our wish to establish the Museum of Fine Arts, he entered into obligations for a further 204,879 florins. (Movement and laughter on Left and far Left. Hear, hear!) ... Indeed, Hon. Members, most of these art objects, together with those previously purchased, were delivered to the gallery. If the situation is favourable, if one can buy really valuable art objects, who could have objections about purchasing these objects, after a National Committee decided that a Museum of Fine Arts should be established, and a certain amount has been made available to buy works of old masters? (Commotion, noise from Left) Please be reasonable, as I am giving you the facts of the matter with complete sincerity. (Lively approval: hear hear!) As you know, the appointment of the present Government was approved approximately at the same time that Cabinet put the 204,879 florins at the disposal of the Minister for Cultural Affairs to go through with the buying transaction. I took over my portfolio perhaps two or three days later.

Before paying for those articles, which were delivered but not yet paid for, I wanted to be certain that they were worthy of the museum. So, on 26.3.1895, about four or five weeks after taking up office, I sent a committee to examine the art collection. The

120

committee, having examined the 256 listed pieces, found that most were reasonably priced. One Russian gallery director, who was on a visit here, offered almost twice the amount of the purchase price.

On the basis of this report, I instructed Károly Pulszky to finalise the transaction. But I did not give him any money. I entrusted Nicholas Szmercsanyi to make payments one by one after obtaining receipts and making sure of every single transaction. Károly Pulszky was then in Italy, and was very offended. He complained to many people that I placed him under Szmercsanyi's supervision; but I felt this to be my duty. I also felt it to be most important that Szmercsanyi should be convinced that the objects were here, and if so, had the previous receipts arrived; and as the receipts arrived he should make the payments one by one. And I dare say, everything went in the greatest order, with the exception of 7,000 florins. Szmercsanyi gave this 7,000 florins to Pulszky because the Director told him that this was for a still outstanding debt, but he was not yet able to obtain the documents; so he had not accounted for this. Everything is accounted for, except the 7,000 florins.

Now, Hon. Members, it is my duty to inform you about the Gallery Scarpa purchase. (Hear, hear!)

This commission was proposed by me. Last autumn Károly Pulszky informed that the contents of the Gallery Scarpa of Lamotta – highly regarded in the art world – were to be auctioned in Milan on the 11th December. I checked the facts, obtained a brochure on the auction, and noticed that the most valuable painting on the list was one considered by some to be by Rafael, by others by Sebastiano del Piombo. The Director of the Gallery asked permission to spend 115,000 florins at this auction. I thought: if we want our Museum of Fine Arts to be up to the highest standard, then if a Titian or a Rafael is available at a public auction which takes place in the presence of a Public Notary, with official documents, then I see my proper duty not to prevent a purchase. Otherwise people would blame me, that a Rafael or a Titian was not bought. I did not want to be responsible for this. (Approval) A public auction is the best way to make certain of the true value and authenticity of a painting – if only we could buy all such paintings at auctions.

So, I put the proposition to a Cabinet Council, explaining just as now, that I could be for ever reproached for not having taken advantage of the possibility of obtaining a Rafael or a Titian at a favourable price, when London and Berlin galleries are not buying just now. Even if that painting is not by Rafael but Piombo. (Commotion on Left) Excuse me, according to experts, it does not make any difference. (Contradiction on Left) Sorry, but you are wrong! I can show the writings of the famous Moselle, who declares the painting to be Rafael's work; on the other hand, Bode claims that Piombo painted it; in which case it is naturally not quite as valuable as if it were Rafael's work, but is still of very great value.

So. When I authorised him in my order No. 59141 to take part in the Scarpa auction, I said, 'Having been convinced of the genuineness and excellent condition of the painting attributed to Rafael, endeavour to obtain it first of all, and if it is available at an acceptable price you may buy other worthy works of art, but only at the auction.' I did not give any other authorisation, and he was not permitted to overspend the grant.

I received a telegram on 15.12.1895 saying that the painting attributed to Rafael was bought at the auction by the Countess Chevigné for 135,000 francs, and that he hoped to take it over from her. At the end of the telegram it said: *I exceeded my commission for a private person.* He probably meant, that because I only authorised him to buy at a public auction, that he overstepped by buying through a private person. But one could have understood that he bought the picture *for* a private person through the Countess Chevigné. I made immediate inquiries as to whether he had overspent the money credited to him. As he did overspend (laughter from the Left) and according to his telegram, he bought the painting from a private person, and not at the public auction, on 30.12.95 I ordered him to report to me in twenty-four hours as a matter of the most urgent responsibility.

He did not return immediately from the auction, but only in December. But as he told me before he left that the Minister for Commerce also entrusted him with some mission, I did not find it suspicious that he was still abroad. When he reported to me, he asked for three more days of respite.

Through private information, I found that the painting attributed to Rafael, together with many other paintings, had already arrived. I realised from this that the purchase executed by the

122

Countess Chevigné was actually done by him, but perhaps he asked her to bid, as he did not want it to be known that the Director of the National Art Gallery of Hungary was the bidder. I thought he might have hoped to obtain the painting cheaper this way.

He has not done his reporting. Consequently, I ordered an investigation. He disregarded my instructions to buy only at the public auction and spend only the amount granted. His actions definitely serve as ground for an inquiry. He exhausted the entire credit.

KÁROLY VÁRÁDY: Honourable Members! I appreciate the fact that the Minister tried to answer my question with sincerity, but regretfully I cannot accept his answer ... One should note that the grant was made in January last year, so the responsibility of the previous Government is in question. That Government resigned on the 29th December or even earlier, and was only a caretaker government in January 1895. So it had no right to make a grant.

The Minister confessed that the Director did not account for 7,000 florins.

Nothing is further from me than to attack anybody personally. I hold the character of everybody concerned in high esteem. But the Hon. Minister's answer crystallises in the fact that the Director had to be under constant control.

What happened proves not only the recklessness of the Director, but the incorrect procedure followed by the Minister.

GZULA WLASSICS: Hon. Members! Excuse me, one must make the purchase when the opportunity offers itself. It is true, there is no legislation, but there is a decision made by the National Committee. Regarding the matter of the 7,000 florins, the Director persevered with his statement that the object had been delivered, but the receipt has not yet arrived, and the amount is for the payment of this particular item. If I had known before the Scarpa auction that this account had not been settled I probably would not have sent him to the auction.

Károly Pulszky addresses the subject (1)

Why is it that the most perfect days
blotch us with discolour?
Energy dissipates, intention slackens.
It is in the moment when purpose
steps away from even our shadow
that you suggest alternatives,
death.
I listen
but I am reminded of language.
You must do
better than that.

1896. February 7th

Report in the newspaper, the *Budapesti Hirlap*

If the Government is interested in the identity of the alleged Countess Chevigné, it would also be advisable to find out to whom did Pulszky send in Paris (six days before he became insane) 8-10,000 florins worth of jewels: a diamond and sapphire brooch and two large earrings.

How interesting! A man constantly struggling with financial difficulties; facing an official inquiry, still takes the time to send such valuable presents to his Parisian girlfriend.

Also interesting, that Ferenc Fenyveri, while visiting Italy shortly after Pulszky's first trip there, heard a lot of suspicious talk from the local antique dealers. On his return he mentioned this to Minister Csaky and also to Pulszky, who reacted with, 'All right, all right! I'll settle it!'

He should have been able to manage on his salary; all the more so as he received an extra 5,000 florins yearly for which he was supposed to give artistic advice to the organisers of the Millennium Exhibition. This has been stopped now, but during the past year he only appeared twice at the organisers' meeting. That is, 2,500 florins per meeting!

The question arises: do we need such a Museum of which Pulszky is dreaming? One in which all the old Schools are represented?

Another question: is Pulszky really such a great expert? Is he really able to judge artistic quality? We are worried that in such haste one could only gather the unwanted and worthless objects in. We have some great artists in this country who are qualified to judge quality. We wonder why didn't the Government ask their opinion, when such large amounts were at stake?

1896. February 8th

Report in the *Budapesti Hirlap*

We have received a letter from a Public Servant, who advises that there has been a general order to Department Heads to watch for drunks and gamblers among subordinates. He wonders if Pulszky's private life is being scrutinised as well; if so, then how come he was entrusted with so much money, when he is in debt up to his neck? in whose home orders of distraint are commonplace, whose private life is so dubious?

The facts released to the press about the midnight consultation on the fourth by famous doctors, were misleading, he reports. The doctors have not found any symptoms to justify a diagnosis of insanity. Furthermore, the sudden consultation was initiated by telephone from the rooms of the Liberal Party!

If we call it a family matter, then this was the Party's and Government's family business.

The diagnosis was intended for the public, but the small inner circle knew very well that the doctors don't know anything about Károly Pulszky.

Today, Dr Salgo explained at length to our reporter why he can't yet have an opinion as to whether Pulszky is insane or not, as classic symptoms are entirely missing.

Károly Pulszky addresses the subject (2)

I have seen you
but only obliquely
as one sees in the grin of a skull
some plan for a face that once smiled.
In my father's museum
there were hints of you in masks,
carvings, terracotta votive figurines.
His concern with ethnological definitions
taught me to look
at the elements and contours in bone.
You are more sardonic than that.

1896. February 9th

Report in the *Budapesti Hirlap*

Today it became certain that the country's money was mishandled, that deceit was committed in all forms; fraud, smuggling and unauthorised buying. But one thing is still not clear. Is Pulszky really insane? Or has he chosen this strange form of suicide to escape the collapse of his house of cards?

Professor Bode, director of the Berlin Museum and one of the world's foremost art experts was asked officially to give information about the Scarpa Gallery. His reply was that the entire Scarpa Gallery has been offered for sale in the past few years, all over Europe, for 100,000 francs, but the owners were unable to find any buyer. But Pulszky paid 135,000 francs for one single painting! In Bode's opinion, this painting (the Piombo) is not worth more than 20–25,000 francs. The art dealer Leitner in Budapest also declared that the whole contents of the Scarpa Gallery was offered to him for 60,000 florins.

Today an elderly Italian art dealer called Sambon appeared at the Parliament looking for Minister Wlassics. He came to collect his money – as others might do after the news of Pulszky's alleged

126

madness reaches Italy. The amount is 17,893 lire for objects which do not seem to be suitable for our Museum: some antique jewellery; Venetian glass, etc. Sambon is prepared to sue. Members in the corridor gathered, and started to question him about the Countess Chevigné, and he obliged.

The Countess is 30 to 35 years old, blonde, of nondescript appearance, and lives on the Boulevard Péreire, the most elegant district of Paris. He did not know if she was married. According to rumour in Budapest, she is identical with one Cléo de Mérode, the infamous Parisian demi-mondaine who caused the rift between King Leopold of Belgium and his wife.

The Countess and her lady companion took luxurious accommodation in Milan and made it known that she was interested in the auction ... When she asked some art dealers to visit her, Pulszky was also present, and they went to the auction together. When it came to paying, the Countess paid cash on the spot, to the amazement of the sellers, who were rather worried about her.

The big scandal has brought other facts about Pulszky to the surface. Namely, a misuse of his position as Director of the National Gallery. Budapest art dealers have been complaining about Pulszky's unfair competition with them. He invited a number of foreign art dealers every year; they used the Gallery rooms free of charge for their dealings, paid no tax after the sales, and no duty for their imported paintings, as these were brought into the country marked for the National Gallery. Pulszky also brought in duty free: clothing, materials, jewels for personal use, but declared them as goods for the National Gallery, they said.

1896. February 12th

Report in the *Budapesti Hirlap*

Pulszky was arrested yesterday. The amount unaccounted for is approximately 56,300 florins.

The Magistrate went to Pulszky's room in the asylum, stated the charge brought against him, and called upon him to confess. Pulszky, with tears in his eyes, said: 'I have not embezzled any money. Everything is in order.'

The two doctors who were present declared that one week was

not long enough to make a definite diagnosis, but he had not shown any sign of great mental disturbance. The Magistrate then announced the arrest.

Pulszky, pale as death and trembling, appealed against this, but was taken to the observation section at the Váci Road Prison. Today he was transferred to the inner city prison and put in a cell by himself.

His appearance has changed dramatically. He asked to see his lawyer friend Krájfsik, who advised him to choose the criminal lawyer, Dr Nagy, for his defence. His friend mentioned that paintings and other art objects worth approx. 10–15,000 florins were found in Pulszky's home which he must have bought for the Museum and apparently forgot to deliver there. Pulszky agreed that this was so, and gave permission to take them to the Museum. His furniture is under no threat of being seized by creditors, as at a previous auction by creditors a relative bought it all, and made a gift of it to young Tessa. This afternoon, all Pulszky's possessions were put in distraint.

1896. February 12th

From records of the Hungarian National Parliament, Parliamentary Session No. 557

AGOST PULSZKY: Hon. Members! I ask permission to speak about a personal question. I was not present at the beginning of yesterday's meeting and therefore I have only now learned the contents of Mr Ferenc Simaz's speech from reading the official report. The Hon. Gentleman said: 'There is a certain sadness about the fact that our fellow Member of Parliament Agost Pulszky, who is the brother of the person in question and who was also Secretary of State at that time, is freely voting in this matter in Parliament.'

In this, Hon. Members, there are two assertions and implications concerning myself; and I owe the house a statement.

Firstly: mention of my being Secretary of State. As I have never in my life tried to avoid total responsibility, I draw the attention of those involved to the fact that two big institutions are led by men who are my closest relatives. So, I accepted my appointment as Secretary of State only and strictly with the stipulation that I would not have any direct or indirect influence on the affairs of these two establishments and that the Ministry would always deal with these, disregarding my person. This was the situation throughout my Secretaryship.

I declare that I had no direct or indirect influence on the affairs of the National Museum of Fine Arts, the Art Gallery, or the National Museum.

Moreover, I had absolutely no knowledge of the affairs of the National Museum of Fine Arts.

The other question that follows from the Hon. Member's statement is on voting on the acceptance of the appeal. I regarded this voting as part of the procedure and order of the House, and not a course to decide the issue. I feel I exercised my right to vote correctly. (Approval from Right)

FERENC SIMAZ: Hon. Members! I wish to say a few words regarding a personal matter. (Noise from Right) As my Hon. Colleague Agost Pulszky's speech was made with reference to my person, you should find it natural that I want to make a personal statement too. (Hear hear!) I find all that my Hon. Colleague has said perfectly correct, and I have never stated that he had meddled in those matters in his official status. Only from the moral point of view regarding public life do I disagree and find it a delicate and awkward situation, that a member of Parliament should take such an attitude and vote against the opposition in such a question.

JANOS FELENYALC: Hon. Members. Undeniably religious affairs were the most important elements for thousands of years in human activity. The ideas of religion had equal influence on the individual, and on all sections of society. The amalgamating influence of religious ideas was felt by the individual, by society and by nations. Since the French Revolution, the ideas of liberty, equality and fraternity were the movers of the mechanism of nations. But in later times production and the big question of Capital are the manipulators of our societies and nations. This new class's first and main God is self-interest. This self-interest penetrates in the individual's emotional and mental life, and manipulates society. This self-interest, be it individual or political party-power interest, is to be found everywhere. It infiltrates the

129

Halls of Legislature, the sanctuaries of religion, and finds its way to the professorial chairs. Its domination is widespread, and society has a name for it: corruption!

We meet this monster in contemporary life everywhere. They say there is corruption in Parliament; corruption in society; corruption in the Art Gallery; corruption in the schools; corruption in the religious denominations; corruption even among the priests. (True! That's so! from far Left) So, nowadays, we speak of little else. The newspapers are full of it: corruption!

As the most important episode of the budget discussion of 1896 the following will be chronicled: the political sea whipped up by the Neptunes of the opposition produces one victim after another. The first victim of corruption was Miklos Gzula, a leader of this corrupted political system; the second man thrown up by these waves was Károly Pulszky, chief of the Art Gallery. He was, for his mad money-sacrifice from the national fortune to purchase beautiful faces and lips by Rafael, first committed to a lunatic asylum, and later as the result of public furore to prison. These whipped-up waves are on the way to bring in other victims. Nobody knows who will be brought to the surface!

1896. February 19th

Report in the *Budapesti Hirlap*

To summarise the Pulszky case: Why was an attempt made, and whose idea was it, to try to declare Pulszky insane? He is now answering questions like the intelligent man he really is. And why didn't his brother, Agost Pulszky, make a decision to pay the missing money earlier and so avoid the entire scandal? Why didn't Minister Wlassics safely and silently, behind doors, deal with the matter – as previous governments always did with all sorts of misdemeanours among their public servants? Was it perhaps because Wlassics wanted to show that the previous government was reckless in handling the country's wealth? – not anticipating he would get into trouble himself.

A friend tells how he kept urging Pulszky to finish the Statement of Accounts, then offered to do it himself, and asked Pulszky for his notes, but in vain.

In the opinion of Károly Pulszky's brother, Agost, he had been in a seriously disturbed state since the 20th of October last year; not being able, for instance, to tell details of his last trip and not remembering what the item was for which he paid 20,000 francs in one of the countries visited.

1897. October 30th

Sitting of the criminal court

At the conclusion of a criminal investigation following the proposal of the Crown prosecutor, the decision was made that: Dr Károly Pulszky born in London; aged 42 years; religion: evangelical; married, with two children; no previous conviction; dismissed from office; having been in custody from 10 Feb. to 7 May 1896 but now at liberty; is charged with official embezzlement. Bail guaranteed. Date of final trial to be fixed. Dr K. P. and Dr Dersö Nagy solicitor notified of their right to lodge an appeal within 8 days.

Reasons for the decision are as follows:

K.P. received 167,000 florins in 1894
               204,000 florins early 1895
               115,000 florins 6.10.1895

               486,000 florins total

As a final part-payment of the 204,000 florins he received 7,000 on 14th Oct. Of this amount he is unable to account for 4,041 florins. From the 115,000 florins he only actually received 113,850 florins (after expenses were deducted by the bank). Of this amount 48,840 florins are missing.

It appears that two art objects are missing. These were allegedly bought in 1895 and there are receipts of 4,000 lire for each.

The accounting of 1895 includes a receipt for payment for 3,500 lire for a painting by Weenix, *The Dutch Family*. The painting was found in the Gallery, but the vendor claims the price was only 1,500 lire. He has not been paid yet.

For the 7,000 florins Pulszky was alleged to buy:

a marble Madonna	1,000 florins
books, reference etc.	2,500 florins
frames etc.	1,500 florins
restoration	2,000 florins
	7,000 florins

The Madonna was bought and is in the Gallery – but Pulszky has not paid for it. No frames etc. were purchased, and no restoration done. Books were bought and paid for 1,538 florins. The accused claims that he bought two paintings on 24 Oct. and has paid for them from the abovementioned monies.

So the missing amount is reduced to 3,691 florins.

Accused denies that he took the money for himself.

At the Scarpa auction he was supposed to buy the portrait attributed to Rafael (Piombo) and a Bacchante attributed to Titian. He spent 141,750 lire on the Rafael (Piombo), and also bought *The Spinner* by Caravaggio for 715 lire and paid for both.

This makes 64,810 florins plus 200 florins travelling expenses. So 48,370 florins are not accounted for.

Pulszky returned from this trip in December and asked for an extra week's leave in January but was unable to render his accounting. On 4th February he was taken to the asylum on the advice of private doctors.

During the investigation the accused claimed that he spent 7,000 florins on duty and delivery fees but can't remember what he spent the rest on.

According to the Statement from Bourgeoise (art dealer, Paris), Pulszky sent him 959 florins to send the so-called Rafael to Budapest. Pulszky also bought from Della Torre (Venice) a stone basin and a stone Madonna for 520 florins, and has paid for these.

On 11.12.95, Pulszky bought a painting attributed to Vittore Beligmino for 3,124 florins. Accused claims to have paid 1,110 lire to M. Giuseppe and part of 3,500 lire to G. Daniano for objects for the Museum of Fine Arts. None of these objects has been found in the Gallery or among the masses of antiquities in his own home. Neither can he say what these objects were.

After final accounting on the above, 47,457 florins remains missing.

The inquiry convincingly proves the fact that Pulszky used the missing money for his own purposes. Pulszky earned 2,500 florins a year, and had a rent-free apartment. This was barely enough for a lifestyle demanded by his social standing and he had no personal wealth. Yet from the Spring of 1895 he was spending lavishly and in a conspicuous manner. Several witnesses have stated that around that time he travelled constantly in coaches, kept a mistress and entertained her, day after day, in nightclubs; went riding daily; took his whole family to Venice, then to Bartfa. There is proof that Pulszky bought for himself a whole Gallery in Massa Superiora for 90,000 lire and paid 5,000 lire advance. He also bought thousands worth of antiques for himself from M. Damiano and made part-payment of large amounts. He also started large-scale costly undertakings and engaged a private secretary to deal with his personal affairs.

All these expenditures came, without doubt, from the 47,457 florins.

During the investigation the entire contents of the National Gallery and the material bought for the future Museum of Fine Arts, as well as all previous receipts, were examined.

Receipts were found for 4,000 lire each for two paintings which could not be found at the Gallery. They are *Saint Jeremiah* by Girolamo, and *Saint Sebastian* by Civerchia. Pulszky claims that he bought the *Saint Jeremiah* in July 1895 from Luigi Resimini in Venice. He knew that the painting is missing and on the list of arriving objects he made the mark 'not here'. He thinks the art dealer might not have sent it, or it disappeared after arrival. Witnesses say it has never arrived. Resimini, art-dealer, swears on oath that he never owned the *Saint Jeremiah* painting and never sold it to Pulszky. Neither had he received the 4,000 lire acknowledged in the receipt, which he made out. He swears he signed it only as a friendly gesture to Pulszky, who asked him to pretend that the transaction took place. Witness Resimini claims that Pulszky told him that he bought a Saint Jeremiah painting somewhere, but had no receipt and he must prove the purchase price.

Despite the denial of the accused, it seems justified to believe that he has produced a receipt for a non-existing purchase.

The other 4,000 lire receipt is about payment for the *Saint Sebastian* bought from R. Marziano in Perugia. The seller testified that this is true, and that together with other art objects he sent it to Wawra, art dealer, in Vienna. He sent 57 cases. Wawra claims that he forwarded 56 cases, untouched, to Budapest to the National Gallery. On the basis of all this, it seems possible that the painting got lost on the way.

During the inquiry a letter arrived from A. Riblet, Florence, complaining that Pulszky took from him in December 1893 a painting by Weenix (Dutch family, the child holding a rabbit). He has not been paid the agreed 1,500 francs. The painting is in the Gallery and did arrive there in 1893. This painting is listed with the accounting of purchases before 24.10.1895 but shown at a purchase price of 3,500 lire, and the receipt is by A. Glisenti from Florence. After declaration under oath by Riblet and another witness it seems that Pulszky took the Weenix painting from Riblet in November 1893 on commission with the promise to sell it. Pulszky insists that he bought this painting from Glisenti for 3,500 lire, but admits he owed 1,500 francs to Riblet for a painting. Glisenti declared he has never seen or sold this Weenix to Pulszky. He sold and received the 3,500 lire for a Van Dyck painting. This painting is in the Gallery, but a separaté receipt for 2,000 lire from Glisenti exists for it, dated 25.8.1895.

It is beyond doubt that the 3,500 lire (= 1,590 florins) has been misappropriated by the accused.

Regarding the transaction at the Scarpa auction, the court accepts that the Countess Chevigné was only involved to keep bidding lower.

Total amount misappropriated by Pulszky, in the light of the above, now stands at 50,902 florins.

Accused endeavoured to cover up his fraud by producing false items and receipts in his accounting to his superiors. The question, as to whether he committed these acts in full control of his mental capacities or otherwise, cannot be decided here. The judge at the final trial will decide that.

Regarding the insanity claim: on 4th February 1895, private doctors ascertained progressive paralytic insanity, but doctors for the court found the accused, after observation, physically and mentally normal. Dr Moracsik thinks some symptoms are suspicious and could mean the start of a mental illness. Ajtay is certain that between August and February 1896 Pulszky was normal. In the opinion of the medical board of the Justice Department there is evidence of a worried state of mind in the summer of 1894, then by the end of 1895 pathological excitement turning to apathy in early 1896. This, aggravated by heavy drinking, shows a case of alcoholic nerve paralysis. The present improvement is probably due to abstinence from alcohol. This opinion was formulated after listening to witnesses to Pulszky's excessive behaviour. Until 1895 Pulszky was an excellent and most careful buyer, did not think it proper to buy similar objects for himself from those he dealt with officially. Witness Peregrini states that Pulszky changed in early 1895, when he started to make purchases and to issue orders without authority; gave contrasting and impossible orders; appeared dishevelled in public; once he let some workmen wait all night; used his office as a dressingroom; installed fountains in the gallery rooms.

Mrs Pulszky told of her husband's sudden rages – he even bit her. He occupied himself with business plans, wanted to build a Parthenon; planned to hold an antique-auction during the millennium celebrations, etc. He made an abrupt decision and took his daughter to Venice to study the zither.

The Ministry of Justice has ordered the medical board to take Pulszky again into observation and, taking into consideration his present condition, to give a new expert opinion.

Drs Olah and Sálgo confirm that the accused's insanity might have developed from alcohol and his psychosis is the megalomanic period of the progressive paralytic insanity. The experts can only base their opinions as to whether Pulszky committed the acts he is accused of, in a state of unaccountability, on the statements of witnesses.

Apart from the fact that every witness is a relative or a friend of Pulszky, they were influenced by the family doctor's opinion on his insanity when they were recalling his earlier extravagant behaviour. His own family doctor and close friend has not observed any strange symptom during the summer and autumn of 1895. Others just remember him as a nervous eccentric.

His mistress in 1895 (Mariska Recsey) never noticed anything abnormal. Several witnesses swore they had never seen Pulszky drunk before 1895. The waiters from the 'Orpheum' said that though Pulszky visited the place every night during the summer of 1895 he was never drunk and only took a little champagne, no hard spirits.

On the 2nd October 1895 Pulszky submitted a detailed account of his purchases earlier that year; a disturbed man could not have done this by himself. At present, his intelligent, clear answers show calm deliberation and a faultless memory. He remembers clearly every item bought for the Gallery and those he bought for himself. When he cannot account for the missing money, he acknowledges the shortage. The fact that he tried to cover up for the shortages by producing false receipts in itself proves his normalcy. The type of insanity the doctors are referring to could not have improved in such a short time. On the contrary, it would have worsened. Usually in two to three years time it ends in death.

Now, after three years, Pulszky shows no symptoms at all. It is well known that Pulszky is exceptionally intelligent, very well educated but very nervy and since childhood rather undisciplined. Every annoyance or disappointment usually puts him in an apathetic condition. The business ventures he was toying with were basically good ideas. The trouble was, he was not a good businessman to follow them through. Properly handled, they would have been very profitable.

Finally, the fact that he bought antiques, a whole Gallery, and several other paintings for himself with the intention of selling them at a profit, shows that he was hoping to pay back the misappropriated money from such income before his deed was discovered.

The Prosecution finds that Károly Pulszky must be charged with official embezzlement.

<hr>

1898. November. Budapest

Emilia Markus receives a visit from her brother-in-law, Agost Pulszky

<hr>

— Emmy. You are looking wonderful, as usual. And the girls, they are enduring?

— But of course. They have suffered from the gossip and the cruelty of friends. Let it strengthen them for later challenges. We still have our circle of true intimates.

— I am sorry if we have lost contact. We did enjoy those parties . . .

— That is over. Agost, it is not a little cruel of you to bring that up. You know precisely the burden of our debts. Why do you think I keep on performing? Everyone marvels at my vivacity, at the youthful charm of my parts. I tell you, it is the most arduous rôle of my life, to be the unruffled loyal wife of a man imprisoned, when even his own family . . .

— Your acting is the toast of Budapest. And your loyalty to Charlie is an added aureole, Emmy. Do you think we do not appreciate that, and admire that?

— Your sister . . .

— Polixena was always Charlie's closest ally, dear Emmy. Do you think that anyone he married would ever overcome a sort of natural jealousy? But I am not here to go over old irritations. You must know, however, just how much we all admire your strength and your courage, these last three years. It seems interminable. All for such a trivial peccadillo.

— Agost, you of all people must be fully aware of the reasons for this almost endless attack upon the Pulszky name. It is hardly Charlie at all, he's simply the scapegoat.

— Poor Charlie, yes. But you cannot make him understand that. I think, in his heart, he would be most affronted to believe that. After all, he must accept that his handling of money matters was pretty hopeless.

— Not at all! If, in the first place, the Minister had given him competent assistance, this would never have happened. And it's not as if Charlie didn't request an assistant. I'm sorry, Agost, that you align yourself with parties that want Charlie to be merely an articled clerk.

— An elementary training in financial principles is hardly outside my brother's intelligence or capacities, Emmy. My God, he had the benefit of my entire Law Faculty at the University, had he requested them! But no, not Charlie. He splashed into the deep end without a thought for consequences, or his family's difficult situation. We all knew the city was full of rivals just ready to plunge a knife in. You can't be a Pulszky and not be aware of that. For ten years now the place has been jammed with spies and pro-Austrian sympathisers, not to mention the entire anti-Semitic push . . .

— Charlie was aware of their hatred. Each time your father published another editorial do you think Charlie did not have to defend it? And he did, I can tell you, with conviction. He admired your father entirely. You don't imagine that duel he fought on your father's behalf was a frolic? I recall it was Charlie, not you, Agost, who rushed in to challenge Várády for deriding the family name . . .

— My parliamentary position, Emmy, forced me to act with restraint.

— Thank God Charlie has never been restrained, then. Even in this, I can still admire his honesty to himself, even if I cannot understand the terrible withdrawal, these long years of almost never speaking. Charlie, who once was so voluble . . .

— The doctors call it a sort of neuresthenia. It is apparently not uncommon in cases of great shock. A sort of defence.

— Against even his family! That is the part the girls find hardest. I find hardest. Yes, I have explained to them. But it is difficult indeed, dear Agost, to deny the deep hurt and the feeling that Charlie in some way blames us, is taking it out on us.

— You have withstood a great deal, Emmy. We all know that, and admire that. I know I do, myself particularly. And of course I'm not insensitive to the political ramifications. In a sense Charlie has called upon himself all the poison that might otherwise have been directed at me in Parliament. And had the Right managed to unseat me it might indeed have ended not only my parliamentary career but our father's entire lifetime of struggle for the Hungarian cause. I am bitter that they could hardly wait until his grave was cold, and Kossuth, who would have supported him and us all, was dead also, before they struck. Poor Charlie, he hardly knew what hit him. None of us did. It's clear enough now. Now it is clear, all right.

— I simply live from day to day. I can do no more. Do you think, Agost, it will ever end?

— You are very brave. You are all very brave. Well, we must make it end. How much is still unpaid?

— I don't know. Forty, fifty thousand florins. It's not even that . . .

— But that is a start. I have been thinking a great deal, Emmy, on ways to get Charlie back to his old self. We know that sending him to London was a disaster. Not only were all the old associations revived, but he could not even undertake the little job as dealer's agent in peace. It only took one old acquaintance from Budapest to run into him – and to quiz him like a hypocrite – and all the good was undone. No. If Charlie is to be helped I think we must get back to essentials, and it has occurred to me that my earlier thinking on the matter of money was not helpful. I mean, Emilia, that we cannot 'teach him a lesson' in the use of money by forcing him, at last, to work off his own debts. No, let me finish. I know your own pride rebels that I should, yet again, come in to his aid like this. But we must think of Charlie. If I were to pay the 50,000 into Treasury it would immediately cut the sniping and rumour and allow the poor man at least the peace to return to Budapest without being ashamed to show his face in any restaurant or eating house . . .

– I will pay his debts. Every one.

– It will take years. As you know, when I inherited the estates I said we would look at possibilities. Well, now all the deeds and transfers are completed: I tell you it can be done. There is no financial embarrassment to me, and as you say yourself, Charlie's suffering is not without congruence to the family name. So you must . . .

– Agost, I am very tired. I have been very tired, and if I do not have my rest this afternoon, tonight's play will be a disaster. Have your will. I take it you have discussed this all with Charlie?

– No, that was not necessary. I wanted to see you. Dear Emmy, it really does pain me that we do not have those wonderful evenings any more. You remember your trick with the painted door?

– Oh my God, why remind me of that? The Desdemona painted on that door is someone far different from the person I am now. I do not think I ever want to look at her again. So unprepared, so innocent, so unaware of the life she had contracted . . . I do the rôle next week . . .

– I know. The last time you performed it, I found it almost unbearably moving. All your performances of late . . .

– Yes yes. They all tell me that. I think, in fact, I have lost something in the rôle. That innocence I spoke about. At a certain stage in one's life innocence is hardly enough. It's what we replace it with that counts. Do you want my personal I.O.U. for this 50,000 florins, Agost?

From records of the Hungarian National Parliament, Parliamentary Session

GZULA WLASSICS: For the unaccounted amount by Károly Pulszky, regarding his commission for the Scarpa Gallery auction, the Treasury received full compensation. (Cries from the Left: Whoever from?)

GZULA WLASSICS: You are aware of the fact that my Hon. Colleague Agost Pulszky made good that loss. Agost Pulszky placed this amount at the Treasury's disposal as a reimbursement for the damage caused by his brother. The loss was paid from this amount. Indeed, as he gave a larger amount than was needed there is a reserve for the use of eventual further damages. (Cries from the Right: Isn't that nice!)

NANDOR HORANSZKY: It should not be accepted! What's all this got to do with Agost Pulszky?

GZULA WLASSICS: Instead of chancing a long and complicated court case I decided to come to an agreement; but so as not to cause any loss to the Treasury. I was willing to cover the costs from money which under different circumstances would have been payable to Károly Pulszky. (Noise on the Left) Such a settlement is preferable to a lengthy court case (Cries on the Left: Who is paying for it?) I am going to tell you. Károly Pulszky is paying the whole amount from lawfully retained salaries.

OSZKÁR IVANKA: Was the Minister Károly Pulszky's lawyer?

GZULA WLASSICS: Excuse me, but when a settlement is the alternative to a court case, I can't see why I should not have accepted the consent of Károly Pulszky's representative to this proposition. I have nothing to hide, I am telling you all! The amount of the settlement is 7,300 florins. This was covered by the retained salary and rent of Károly Pulszky, who was acquitted by the criminal court on the ground of diminished responsibility. We also have the remaining surplus money given by Agost Pulszky, for damages occurring from the Scarpa auction. You will remember that I initiated the criminal charge after failing to receive accounting for the Scarpa auction . . .

ISTFVAN RÁKOVSKY: This was correct!

GZULA WLASSICS: Whether it was right or wrong, I will not discuss that. But it was my duty. It was certainly correct that the results of the criminal procedure and the content of the judgment should serve as guidelines to proceeding by the Public Administration. (Approval on Right; noise on Left: That is not so!) Please hear me out before judging. In February 1896, I suspended Károly Pulszky from office and retained ¾ of his 2500 flr. salary, leaving him ¼ for provisions. This is according to the current Civil Service Act the correct, accepted procedure. Now, the High Court and the King's Bench both dismissed the criminal charge with the justification that it had been proved that Károly Pulszky was not capable of rational conduct at the time of the offences.

NICHOLAS BARTHA: That's when he was trusted with half a million?

GZULA WLASSICS: We did not entrust him at all with half a million. I have told you what I authorised him to do. I authorised him to make a purchase at the Scarpa auction. It is quite clear that no loss has resulted from this.

NICHOLAS BARTHA: Yes – when he was mentally disturbed!

GZULA WLASSICS: Well, according to the Hon. Member Istfvan Rákovsky, he has seen how 'healthy' Pulszky is now; but when the authorisation was given, neither my predecessor nor I had noticed anything, otherwise he would not have been given a commission. I was notified of the judgment on the criminal case. Then I initiated disciplinary procedure. The opinion of the disciplinary council was that he, Pulszky, cannot be dismissed. (Laughter on far Left; approval on Right) He cannot be dismissed because he was mentally disturbed when he committed the acts for which a disciplinary action resulting in loss of office could be ordered. We are confronted with *Res judicata*.

OSZKÁR IVANKA: That was cleverly arranged!

GZULA WLASSICS: I beg your leave, if you will consider the matter calmly you will find it impossible for a Minister to contradict the ruling of the criminal court. (Movement and contradiction on Left and far Left)

OSZKÁR IVANKA: You know all the tricks!

GZULA WLASSICS: The truth is that if we stamp on such legal rulings, then all trust in jurisprudence will be shaken. The question is not whether he is affected by mental disorder at the present; but only the fact that according to the presented medical certificate he was not, then, fit to continue service.

ISTFVAN RÁKOVSKY: In the introduction to his speech the Hon. Minister for Cultural Affairs defended the courts. I know very well that the courts have based their rulings on the opinion of the Board of Health, which pronounced Pulszky to be suffering from 'progressive paralysis'. I have attacked this because I don't believe it to be thorough or correct. The fact that Károly Pulszky is staying at the present in London and works as an Antique Dealer's agent proves it. If he is capable now of doing this, then probably he would have been fit to atone for his deed. But Hon. Members, it is rather strange that the Hon. Minister told us that it was proved at the time the crimes were committed Pulszky was suffering from progressive paralysis, that is, he was mentally ill. And just as the court established this fact, the Minister authorised him to make such important purchases.

GZULA WLASSICS: Me? Certainly not! (Contradiction on Right)

ISTFVAN RÁKOVSKY: Well, then the other Minister! Don't be so delighted, Kálman Szentivanyi in particular! (President rings bell) If Károly Pulszky was really mentally ill, then it is most cruel to deprive him of his superannuation. (Noise) This superannuation was used to give back books he bought and so the difference was paid from the State's money. The resulting shame is ours, for free.

Károly Pulszky addresses the subject (3)

Thank you, death,
I did not suggest
a time for anything.
In my father's museum
so many death offerings smiled.
The skull intends us
to achieve something like satisfaction.
You were right.
Nothing costs what we are prepared to give.
Nothing we are prepared to give acquires permanence.
Permanence (you grin) is nothing.
Not permanence, but barter. You have all the cards.
You don't need them.

Defence lawyer Dr Nagy states his reasons for appealing against the charge of embezzlement in the matter of Károly Pulszky

From the beginning, this case has transgressed the limits of ordinary judicial proceedings. It became entangled in party-political viewpoints. It was discussed in Parliament; in the press and at meetings everywhere. The sensational subject excited public opinion and saturated it with misconceptions. Strong political passions led to sharp attacks against the medical board of the Justice Department. The air was filled with suspicion against everybody connected with the case, thus helping the prosecution.

The defence must start with the mental state of the accused, because only then can we find the reasons for his acts, and resolve whether they are criminal or not.

The Court abstains from the opinion of the medical forum, and refuses to make a decision about the question of mental health, leaving that to the Judge at the final trial. Surely it can not be the prosecution's or the judge's rôle to attempt to make a better diagnosis than the doctors, who have spent their lives studying and observing such illnesses? The law has only the right to decide whether the diagnosed mental illness constitutes unaccountability or not. This case has been dragged through publicity for years – what's the use of taking it to a final trial? After the medical board ordered a new observation period the two court psychiatrists still adhered to their original contrasting opinions. The medical board of the Justice Department then formed its final opinion that the accused was suffering from mental illness at the critical time.

The members of the board have been exposed to attacks from the party-press when they gave their first verdict, but they have maintained their ruling, disregarding the consequences. These doctors have the highest professional standards in the country and there is absolutely no reason to doubt that they have done their duty conscientiously and true to their oath. What new result could be obtained by a final trial? None! It's not likely to be held without the medical experts, whose opinions will not change. Neither will the witnesses change their stories. A resolution to discontinue the case should be made now. Of the two court doctors, Mocavcsik is a first-class authority as a psychiatrist; the other doctor excels in other fields. The medical board has the best psychiatrists in the country among its members. Now, if the Court could not trust their judgment, the logical step should have been to call in the best experts from other countries. Instead, the law was trying to play at being medical experts.

According to the prosecution, the experts who diagnosed mental illness have been using different terminologies when naming the illness. This does not mean that they are talking of a different illness, but hat the same illness has different names in its early or late stages.

During Pulszky's stay in the asylum a considerable remission took place, and so far no worsening has followed. This only means that the mental illness has not yet reached the stage where it cannot retrogress. This is the stage called by medical science 'pseudo-paralysis', or 'megalomaniac state' – which can be healed, but under unfavourable conditions may worsen again.

So, because the accused did not die after two years – his condition has improved instead – the prosecution thinks he could not have been ill at all.

This is the layman's opinion against the experts' conviction. This layman's disbelief was strengthened by the fact that the accused behaved perfectly normally during the investigation and declared himself to be healthy. The medical board finds this fact rather worrying and calls it dissimulation. The real mental patient tries hard to dispel the suspicion of mental illness, and doesn't believe he is ill. Now the accused could easily have produced a few symptoms for the prosecution, like trembling, speech difficulty, etc., to convince them; but no, he makes no effort at all to get out of his perilous situation. For one and a half years he sits patiently in a sanatorium, hardly sees even his family. Doesn't think of escaping, but quietly waits for his trial, and plans afterwards at the age of 45 or 50 to leave his family and his country and go to Japan or Africa or wherever and start a new life. Such a thought can only be the product of a sick mind, being in complete contrast with one's normal instinct for self-preservation.

The prosecution thinks that all the business matters attempted by the accused were good ideas. Maybe so, but each venture demanded a whole person's attention full time; and Pulszky lost his judgment completely. This is typical of megalomania. He attempts impossible tasks, but instead of working on fulfilling them, he plunges himself into sexual and alcoholic excess, thinking himself to be the greatest of men.

The prosecution's most serious argument against illness is that the accused was able to hand in his accounting in September 1895. There are many similar cases where insane people have handled great amounts of money successfully, or handled important papers.

The facts about the alleged embezzlement:
The most important point to stress is that the accounting between the parties has been already settled. There is no missing money.

Let me repeat: there is no money that is unaccounted for any more or which is outstanding. Therefore, no further infringement of the law exists.

Consequently there is no case for either civil or criminal procedure. For this reason even the question of Pulszky's mental state also becomes redundant, irrelevant.

But let me summarise: the commission to make the purchases was given to Pulszky the private man, the excellent expert. Nothing was publicised for the simple reason that prices would have doubled or trebled if news of the intended Museum of Fine Arts interest leaked out. So, the money transaction was more a private than an official one between the Minister and Pulszky.

Pulszky admits that 40,902 florins were unaccounted for, but denies that he used this money for his own purposes, and denies the act of embezzlement. This case is different from other ordinary cases: politics have interfered with it. It gave an excellent opportunity for the Opposition to blow it out of all proportion.

We must therefore demand the restitution of judicial power which constitutes permanency and stability and safeguards the life, honour, liberty and property of citizens.

The State hasn't suffered any damage so there is no cause to bring action for embezzlement. But if – incredibly – the Court should still take the stand that even after the missing money has been paid it must find out what happened to this money, it will not be able to prove misappropriation. Károly Pulszky is an excellent expert but totally unsuited to handle money. He was given the task of looking after half a million. At the same time he must travel all over Europe, bargain with art dealers and agents; concentrate to make the right artistic decisions; be a businessman, cashier, transporter and accountant. He had Szálay to help him for about two weeks, then he was left alone again. He mentioned to Szmercsanyi that he wished he could have been with him from the start, as he cannot handle money very well, not even his own. He has asked the Minister for assistants to handle the money as he was uncomfortable about the large amounts. Criminals seldom ask for inspectors. His fate has a disturbingly tragic element. Those nominated to be his supervisors and helpers don't take their jobs seriously and abandon him, and he, carrying the seed of a developing mental disorder, is left alone to roam through Europe with all that money. Even if we don't call it mental illness, but just great nervous tension and excitation, overburdened with the problems and responsibility, we cannot expect from him the same punctuality with figures as from an accountant who has nothing else to worry about but figures.

One must look at the methods of selling art in Italy. Usually it's done by families through agents. These have to be tipped to get good service. Export licences must be obtained somehow, as exporting of art objects is prohibited otherwise. So it's money, money, at every step. Difficult to remember how much and where it was spent while a person concentrates on highly intellectual work. Would Károly Pulszky at the start of the realisation of his dream, the Museum of Fine Arts, destroy everything, himself and his family by stealing 50,000 florins? Impossible.

Now let's look at the so-called extreme lifestyle.

First: taking his family to Venice and Bartfa. Pulszky's wife the great actress has an income of 12,000 florins plus earnings from guest appearances. She doesn't need stolen money to have a rather inexpensive holiday. Besides, in the summer of 1895 Pulszky had not even received the amounts he was supposed to misappropriate. He needed a coach in August for just two weeks, being very busy with the historical exhibition. This could not have cost more than 200 florins.

For his riding he used a friend's horses. But even to hire a horse would only cost two florins per day.

Mariska Recsey, his mistress, received only 400 florins. This association and the night-clubbing stopped right after he received the critical amount. The business ventures did not pass the planning stage, there is no proof of any money being involved.

He employed a secretary only for three months, at 60 florins monthly pay.

All of these items could have cost only about 2,000 florins.

Apart from his regular income he had supplementary honorariums from his writing and he received 5,000 florins for his work with the millennium exhibition; his wife also contributed largely to household expenses.

He went abroad immediately after receiving the critical 7,000 and 115,000 florins, from which he supposedly took the 50,000 florins. He left Budapest on the 24th of October 1895 for Cologne, Paris, London, Milan, Brussels, then back to Paris, Venice, Milan, Rome and Venice once more. He spent two to three days in each place. An exhausting itinerary. After arriving home in December, he spent his days in bed, mostly asleep, before entering the asylum. The 50,000 disappeared between October and December, so it could not have been spent on those activities mentioned by the prosecution.

The accused cannot give any explanation.

It is possible that while travelling in trains and carrying this large amount, the money was stolen from him, or he might have lost it. Whatever has happened, one may call it carelessness but not misappropriation. It may call for a civil lawsuit for damages, but not for criminal charges.

One could suppose that he hid the money, but then he would not have returned. One more possibility exists. Malignant international crooks took advantage of his mental state and exploited him, taking money in advance for transactions which have never eventuated. Such were the purchases from the Gallery of Massa Superiora, the Schmidt-Maref Gallery in Nice; the library in Udine and purchases in London at the firm Colnaghé. Incomprehensible that Pulszky could acknowledge all these as business transactions for himself. This is insanity.

The Court's conclusion regarding the Saint Jeremiah and the Weenix family painting rests on misunderstanding. The Weenix painting: accused bought two rather similar paintings from the Dutch school. Van Dyck family with horse. The receipt for 2,000 lire describes the subject in an unmistakable way. The other painting: family with rabbit by Weenix. The receipt by Glisenti for 3,500 lire also describes the subject. These receipts were correct and genuine, and the monies were paid for these paintings.

Glisenti said in court that he thinks he never saw the Weenix with rabbit, and he never owned it. Glisenti's mixed-up statement must have been influenced by rumours spread in Italy about the case. The agents were alarmed by the thought that they might get into trouble also. There is no proof that the Weenix taken from Riblet is the one with the rabbit. Many paintings are copied and the owners usually insist that theirs is the original. When Riblet inspected the Weenix he said that it was ruined by an unskilled renovator who polished it, and now it is slightly different from what it was before. Riblet was mistaken. This was not the same painting he gave Pulszky, as it has never been polished by the Gallery's renovator. Riblet also said that his painting was signed and dated, but the one in question was only signed.

The *Saint Jeremiah*: the accusation that such a painting was never bought and that Resimini gave Pulszky a false receipt as 'a friendly gesture' is based solely on Resimini's statement. Resimini is a seventy-five-year-old third-rate agent. He was willing to accuse himself with supplying a false receipt because he was afraid that he might be asked to pay the price of the lost painting. His statement does not deserve any credence. Hundreds of cases were packed and unpacked by the Italian agents.

Pulszky trusted them, he was never present at the packing and carting of consignments. How easy to omit one painting and even to resell it to someone else. The Court has accepted the fact that the *Saint Sebastian* was lost in transit. This must have happened to the *Saint Jeremiah* also.

Finally, the case for the defence calls for a true judgment. We plead with God to keep the judges unpolluted by the air saturated with political terrorism in this case.

'In the valleys of the Karpathians we often meet with lakes of immeasurable depth. Through these lonely pools no springs visibly gurgle up; from them no living rivulets emerge. The lake is silent as its surrounding dale: and did not the sun's heat draw off the waters in copious stream, they would inundate the narrow meadow, by which they are bordered on one side, or the strong walls of rock against which they splash with monotonous uniformity.

'. . . At the clear green lake, near the summit of Lomnicz, even the dark vegetation of the fir-tree has already failed. Scanty mountain-pines and mosses might seem to be the sole representatives of the magnificent family of plants, did not the Alpine-Rose, that lovely companion of the chamois, here and there soften the wild prospect . . . Barren, however, as were those regions, they were beautiful with a purple light, which softened the edge of the rugged rock, and shed mild brilliance over the dreariest mountain side, even when the sun had disappeared . . .

'The cause of this heavenly beauty was no secret to the Karpathian peasants. They knew that on the brow of a precipice, which almost reached to the level of eternal snow, a *Carbuncle* lay, imbibing all day long the sun's unveiled glances, and radiating them forth again at night on the whole country around. This wonderful stone was so magnificent, that its renown necessarily spread all over the world. Many a king had heard of it, and promised half a kingdom to him who would lay the celebrated gem on the steps of the throne.

'The prospect of such a reward excited more than one fearless man to the enterprise, but in vain. Like polished marble, the rock offered no projection to the ascending foot. No one could approach the shining jewel, which lay aloft, beyond the flight of the arrow, or of the eagle. Its purple rays continued to illumine the lovely nights of the unpeopled valley, as if it disdained the palaces of kings; and every attempt to reach it failed.

'A sportsman had for years and years longed to climb up to this virgin summit. He vied with the chamois, and even surpassed

149

its danger-despising alertness, but remained ever far from his aim. At last he resolved to try with his rifle to win the treasure he was unable to grasp. He chose to expose the precious stone to be scattered in pieces, rather than renounce its possession; for he knew that every fragment of it would prove of priceless worth. But his new mode of attack had no better success than before; his balls rebounded from the rock, and fell flattened to the ground; none attained to the height of the Carbuncle.

'But the heart of the sportsman was bent upon his purpose. He would not recede, and pledged his soul to the Demon for a "Free Shot". The "Free Shot" is a tradition well known by German and Hungarian sportsmen. The devil, called upon by the sportsman, grants to him six balls, which cannot fail their aim, but the seventh ball belongs to the devil, and he directs it according to his own choice.

'At dusk he hastened to the lake. His sight was dazzled by the golden twilight around. He trembled as he drew the trigger, yet his aim could not fail. The ball precisely hit the point in which the gem was joined to the rock; but the power of the shot was too great. It severed the Carbuncle from the granite, but instead of precipitating it on to the meadow, which lay between the rock and the water, hurled it into the waves of the bottomless lake.

'Whereupon the "Eye of the Sea" grew dark, and since that time it reflects only the barren rock, being no longer brightened by the Carbuncle. The secluded dale is disturbed no more by the cupidity of men, for its treasure has vanished.'

(from *Tales and Traditions of Hungary*,
Francis and Theresa Pulszky)

1970. Los Angeles

Romola Nijinsky recalls her family

Budapest. London. Brisbane. Did you know my family? Yes, you are thinking of my husband. Poor Vaslav. He has become one of the myths of our century.

My father, did you know he was also an important man? I often wonder, had he lived, what would have been my own growth and

150

direction? How would he have tempered the fine coiled spring that was my mother? I am told that he gave magnificent parties, it was perhaps one of the sadder things my mother learned from him. Budapest in its day was indulgent to a degree. My father and his own father, Ferenc Pulszky, were purists. They were naive enough to believe in some redeeming concept of 'good' that transfigured their petty indulgences. Is it true that they saw art only as a key to the other spoils of privilege? I cannot believe it. My own father wrote me stern injunctions to study, even in his final letter.

In old age I imagine him lean and ascetic, like those last photographs of Dreyfus, do you know them? My father would have recognized Vaslav. Were he alive he may have helped.

Why do I mention Dreyfus? Their fates were too dissimilar; Dreyfus was narrow ... but did you know a strange thing, a coincidence? On the very day my father, in his exile, ended it all – it was in 1899, the 5th of June – on that same day Captain Dreyfus on Devil's Island received the telegram that brought him out of his exile, and back into the world. I was taught to note such things.

I often think of my father, and how his life might have been changed had he known of the Dreyfus reprieve. The newspapers of all the world were full of the affair, it must have been gossip even in Brisbane.

How selfish a thing suicide is. A year, another two years – a month, a week, and he would have realised that. It is a thought that comes to each of us.

Nobody loses their name entirely.

My father who died thinking he had betrayed his family died only because he had lost a vision and had no other to replace it, though he had reached a strange new land that could have been full of possibilities. We carry our own possibilities within us.

I had a dream last night in which a white deer came to drink from a fountain. It was in an enclosed garden. Its antlers were of rapiers but I was not afraid. Like the fabulous Lady of the Unicorn, I let it approach. I held out my hand. I protected it from the hunters and from the slavering monstrous dogs. They were the most fearful. I held it in the protection of my walled garden. 'Tell me your fear,' I soothed it. 'Tell it to me.' In my walled garden it was not free, now, but it was no longer savaged. If only my father had conceived a dream like this. It was he who first gave me the myths of hart, stag, unicorn. When he rode in his mad, passionate way, as a child I thought of him as an antlered stag.

Yes. You are thinking of my husband. I was talking of him too, poor walled captive. It is so sad that the dream never occupies what we dreamed; that the reality does not hold us with comfort. It is as if we lived in two places. Do you think, in his exile, my father ever dreamed what my future might possibly be?

'I had made friends in Paris with a young Hungarian, Romola de Pulszky, who had had some lessons with Maestro Cecchetti. She was very beautiful, elegant and cultivated, and I was delighted to hear that she was coming with the company to South America. I used to love Romola having her glorious ash-blond hair (natural!) brushed by her Hungarian maid, while we had endless talks about Nijinsky, whom we both adored . . .

'In the last week Nijinsky told me, almost as a joke, that he was in love with Romola. I asked what language he talked to her, for she had no Russian and his French was so primitive.

' "Oh, she understands everything," he said, smiling wistfully.

'I did not believe it was serious. We all knew he was Diaghilev's lover. But when we arrived in Rio we spent a whole day on shore, he alone with Romola and the rest of us in groups . . . Later, in the evening, I went out on the empty deck and stood bending over the rail longing for the ocean to swallow me. And yet that very moment saved me from the bitter life of Romola, whom I so envied then . . .'

(from *Quicksilver*, Marie Rambert)

'Those who heap the blame on Romola Nijinsky are wrong ...
She stubbornly refused to recognize failure after failure, and,
unconsciously, she hastened the onslaught of the tragedy. But her
blindness was the blindness of love. And her love, after those first
short months of happiness, endured painful ordeals; it survived
the grievous trial of a long life ... This eccentric and extravagant
woman did herself perform miracles of patience, devotion and
courage.'

(from *Nijinsky*, Vera Krasovskaya)

1981. Gold Coast, Australia

The tenor Josef Halmos remembers Kyra Nijinsky living in Florence in 1946

When I knew Kyra she was slim, so slim, like a boy. She was very
intense, very beautiful. Fiery. She burned like a fire. Igor
Markevich divorced her because he said she was insane. She was
so intense, she was so very intense, and she had great gifts.

Her gifts were too many. So many directions: ballet, at first.
She became very famous until she was in her late twenties. Of
course her father's name was a great help, and he had seen his
talents transferred to her, as a child. He had said that. But she
painted also, she wrote poetry in seven languages. She was interested in everything. That was her problem.

Too many directions. But by the Second World War she had
begun to do choreography. It is perhaps a pity that her father's
system of choreographic notation was not finished, designs for
dance are forgotten so quickly. I think she had disagreements
with everyone.

She started teaching ballet in Florence, in those post-war years.
She was rushed with pupils. None of them lasted a year; she
demanded perfection. Yes, she was mad, in a way. So intense, she
was so intense.

Almost her father alive again, though he was still alive somewhere. She was close to her father, but she and her mother,
Romola Pulszky, did not get on. They lived apart from her

153

infancy. Her sister, Tamara Nijinsky, also, Tamara was brought up by her grandmother, Emilia Markus in Hungary. Romola Nijinsky-Pulszky was very rich and had houses in Rome, London, Switzerland, America, I think even in Japan. But she never gave Kyra any financial assistance at all. When I knew Kyra in those difficult Florence years she was separated from Igor Markevich (who had a cottage on the Berenson estate). She had only one studio-room in the heart of the old city. It was rented.

I remember the first time I met Kyra. She was very strange, it was in a restaurant in Florence. I met her through a mutual friend, an Hungarian painter. She had a ring which she said was inherited. A sort of snake of gold with a jewel, a topaz I think. If anyone came into the restaurant she could look into her ring and tell all the private details of that person – how old, how many children, his health, his problems, anything. She told me all my private life, looking into that ring. She had occult powers. It was surely her, not the ring.

And now I have just seen Kyra on television with Margot Fonteyn. I was staggered. I did not recognise her. She looked, in her late sixties, more like her grandmother, the Hungarian actress Emilia Markus in old age – that broad face, massive and large. When I knew her she was slim as a boy.

No, she did not speak to her mother. Did you know George Lifar had a monument to Vaslav Nijinsky erected, through subscription, on Nijinsky's grave in the Paris cemetery, and that Romola would not put in anything towards it. When she died she was buried there beside Vaslav. Monuments last such a long time. Here is a photograph of Kyra. That is the way I would remember her.

1944. April

Vaslav and Romola Nijinsky flee Budapest

'It was Easter Sunday ... in the valley we could see the Soviet troops streaming towards the west like the advance of Genghis Khan, a most gruesome and magnificent sight. Thousands and thousands of tanks, heavy guns and cavalry, covered by hundreds of planes, rolled along through the green smiling spring country-side.

'Within a few hours the town [Sopron] was occupied, the forest and all the houses were invaded. The Russian soldiers came into the houses in small groups.

'Our gates were broken down and three tall young Russians carrying automatic machine-guns entered our house.

' "Nemetzki, Nemetzki!" they shouted loudly.

'In a moment everybody in the house fled, panic-stricken, behind curtains and beds. Only Vaslav remained quietly lying on his couch while I stood beside him. The Russians shouted at me, "Nazi?"

'Vaslav, unexpectedly shouting still louder, replied in Russian.

' "Keep quiet!"

'The soldiers stood dumbfounded and lowered their automatics.

' "A Russian? How does he come here? Is he a prisoner?"

' "Yes, he is my husband, an artist." I did not know that I had pronounced a magic word.

'Next morning two trembling Hungarians in plain clothes arrived.

' "We are detectives and were sent here to fetch you. We are sorry but can't help it. You have to come down to the Komman-datura."

'Pavel shivered in his bed.

' "Don't go, they will kill you."

'The three old ladies and Bozsi, the caretaker's wife, began to cry and said farewell to me. Bozsi volunteered to come with me, but the detectives refused to allow him.

' "We have strict orders only to bring down the lady," they said.

' "You can follow, but you can't go to the building of the Kom-mandatura; even we are not allowed to enter."

'Vaslav was still asleep.

' "Let me first quickly prepare his breakfast, and then let us hurry – I want to be back before my husband awakes."

'The detectives looked at me with astonishment, but gave per-mission. I could see by their expressions that they did not believe that I would ever return.

'Never in my life had I gone so fast down the hill to Sopron. Whatever awaited me, I wanted to get it over quickly. Everything

I had read or heard or seen in films in the past about Russia and its regime whirled around in my thoughts. The town was completely changed. The streets were full of Russian soldiers, tanks and lorries everywhere, horses grazing in the gardens, doors broken down. Those houses which still had windows had them wide open. Before the hospital, stretchers were laid out with wounded soldiers, and from every house the sound of wireless was pouring out in an indescribable medley of sound, playing Tchaikowski, Rimsky Korsakov and Strauss waltzes. No Hungarians were in sight. Sopron had become a Russian town overnight.

'The detectives handed me over to the sentinel in front of the Kommandatura, who called another soldier who told me to follow him . . . I had the feeling of being lost in an unknown world. Finally, I entered a small room. There was a large desk covered with papers, and a bed on which was hastily thrown parts of a uniform, an astrakan cap and a sword. The wireless played *Thamar* by Balakirev. I thought, what a long way I had gone since that early spring day in 1912, when I first heard this music at the Russian ballet.

'A tall handsome officer entered, spotlessly attired. I noticed that he must be of high rank, judging by the heavy gold braid and badges he wore on his shoulders. My escort saluted and left us. The officer sat down and scrutinised me.

' "You live in this town, are you a native?" he asked in broken German.

' "I was born in Budapest," I replied in Russian, "My parents were Hungarian. We came here only about a year ago to hide, as my husband has been suffering from a mental illness since the First World War, when we were prisoners in Hungary too."

' "Your husband is incapable of work? What was he?"

' "He is an artist, a dancer, born in Kiev and was a member of the Opera House in St Petersburg."

' "When did he leave Russia?"

' "In 1911. He was sent with the Russian Ballet on a tour through Europe and later to America." . . .

' "Your name?"

' "Romola Carlovna Nijinskaia."

' "What you say? Nijinskaia?" He closed his eyes for a second and murmured "Nijinskaia" and then suddenly, as though struck by lightning, he straightened up, threw his pencil on the desk, and dashed out of the room.

156

'I waited. An hour must have passed . . . the door opened suddenly and the officer entered, accompanied by an older one of higher rank. The newcomer sat down at the desk while the younger one pushed a chair towards me saying, "Saditze pajalusta".

'I sat down.

' "You claim to be the wife of Nyezsinski, our great dancer, who with Chaliapin showed the western world our art?"

' "Yes."

' "The man you are hiding is your husband, I understand. He became ill after the first war, and you were prisoners in both wars here in Hungary?"

' "Yes."

' "Where have you lived since the last war?"

' "In Hungary, Austria, France and Switzerland. We were going from country to country in search of a treatment to restore my husband's health."

' "Your husband was unable to work? Who looked after him during these twenty-six years?"

' "I did."

' "What is your profession?"

' "I haven't one. I was brought up as most other society girls, a general education, chiefly the arts and music."

' "So how did you provide for both of you?"

' "At first I used the funds my husband gave me which he earned while he was dancing. Later, when I saw that the doctors' fees, treatments, and nursing homes would swallow all our savings, I began to write, lecture and work for films."

' "You mean you had to pay for the nursing homes and doctors?"

' "Yes."

' "During the twenty-six years, no government paid for him, none of his colleagues provided for his care?"

' "No."

'The Commandant turned round, gave just one look at his aide-de-camp and spat on the floor.'

(from *Nijinsky*, Romola Nijinsky-Pulszky, pp. 510-14)

157

Part VI: Canticle

Katie Damrow remembers being sent to collect firewood around Myrtletown in June 1899

I know the place. I have been taught some things, you know. Papa showed me first but Alfie Taggart found the best place. There's tinderwood. There are bouncy mats in the ti-tree scrub like a mattress, Alfie says. He showed me then we played touching. Mats of needles and soft leaves. He rolled me there and it didn't hurt. I promised papa I would look for tinder. I don't know why I went back again.

I don't know why I ran. The man was dead. The blood and bits at the front where the flies were didn't make me spew. I thought of that big toad the Bain kids stuck on the barbed-wire fence when it was still alive. I thought of it how it looked next day. Not only flies but birds pecking, crows and seagulls. They eat anything. Of course I ran, didn't I run!

I looked for just one bit at his face. Not like the toad at all, at least the face.

The Inquest was all police and officers asking me. What could I say? It was only when they said the things he owned like that snake jeweled armlet. Wished I looked more. Papa hasn't discovered the gold sovereign. I'll hide that till I marry. Till I'm gone. Dead men are nothing. His eyes were open. He was looking at me. But Yah!, I thought, you can't do nothing.

But I was glad the crow and the seagull were first. I'll buy something so big they'll all hate me see if I care. I'll buy a steamer and sail away to - - to Moongalba pier.

A Canticle for Károly Pulszky

Inscription, plot U835, Toowong Cemetery, Brisbane, Australia:
  In memory of Charles Pulszky
  Born in London 10th Nov. 1853
  Died in Myrtletown 5th June 1899.

My hiding place is the Old Law,
I hide in songs.
              Stork, stork,
              Why are your feet bleeding?

Someone said the name 'Budapest'. As if
my neck snapped, each syllable is an antler.
Indifferent Budapest jerks the tic
of my pulse. It takes time to falsify.
It takes all my time
to admit my passport tells lies
in attempting to name me. I have a signature:
it's dishonoured.
              My neck did not snap,
you understand, I am legally unimpeached.
The enchanted stag broke from the resting-place
and I sailed, my own exile, to the rim
of Australia where nothing's
the same. Can we know loss if we are not deprived?
Stab-jerks, twitch, pain with its compelling
little curiosities —
        I look outside through glass already dusted
        the air is sullen like animal breath
        there is a street of picket fences
        wooden cottages raised so they thump the wind
        on forest stumps. They are no fairytale.
        I look out to the impacted clay
        of a new city and notice
        a parasitic fig sprouting out of a gutter.
        My room takes no time to instruct me

162

all the accustomed shapes are wrong.
It forces me to retain fingerprints.
To have a past, to have losses. Wrong. Wrong.

If I die before you, love, will you cover my body with your
shroud?

I will bequeath hunger. No tears; beneath a log
smirking with fungus I am observed. Snakes eyes lack tears.
Something moves, grass mottles like deerflanks, stones
click without tongues.
*   I could not ask, so they gave me*
a signature, it is called distance, it is said to be
indifference but it's something that moves and is unquenchable.
The signed was impressed at birth, it is named the Old Law.
I have no choice in it.

Deposition of John Bain on oath, Police Court, Brisbane 10th Day
of June A.D. 1899:
   I am the licensee of the Hotel at Myrtletown. I remember Tuesday last the sixth of June. I saw Acting Sergeant Jennings on that
day. He asked me to look at the dead body of a man. I saw the
man the day previous. He came into my bar and had two drinks,
they were shandygaffs. He was quite sober. He told me he was
travelling for the A.M.P. Society, he asked me to insure my life
with him.

'. . . the enchanted stag lured Nimrod's sons, Hunor and Magor,
through treacherous swamps until they reached a land of exceed-
ing beauty, abundant in fish and game . . . here the white stag
leaped into a pond and disappeared forever . . .'

Did I have a wife once? I sleep alone, a snake coils
at the wound and drinks its fill. Jewel eyes hold
indifference brilliantly, tongue functions, rapid,
without moisture almost without feeling. She says
these eyes are my own but I look back at her.

Twigs dry-snapping, shrunken heat – too much light?
Can there be drowning in light?
                          This end of the curve,
Brisbane, what does it know about ends? It tells me
it is learning to listen and I think:
antler-thump.

Each tree shreds itself, light plunges — antlers.
Treetrunks bark-torn — antler rage.
Tussocks uprooted — antlers.
That echo knocking against rockface — antlers,
antlers.
Glare, everywhere — milky eyes in rut
of the white antlered stag. I am just one step
out of danger.

The signs tell me I am surrounded by men who have scraped
all marks off. In my stained palm a small daughter (Romola)
discovers softness, has a claim, wears me as those gloves
her mother may not recover.
                          The charge was not 'misappropriation'
but 'appetite'. I had so much to give I left seedhusks
like the parasite fig. Emilia, wife, remind them of that.
I forged love, Emmy, ambition, perhaps no one is guilty.
All learning comes to artifice, forgery. Tongues dry out
here. Or swell
into fungus. Do not believe my disbelief.

That enchanted stag came to sour country at its edges.
Flat, last outreach, it is called 'the Bay'
and it bears a forged name, Myrtle Town.
Three tree-stilt houses on chicken-legs. The great plain.
A calm. I am calm. A snake eyes me among crow-birds,
white gulls. All share the sheen of decay. Heat
refracts this into dust. I pull that onto my fingers.
I followed, father. I will not be your hostage.

Charles Campbell Jennings on oath saith:
    About a mile and a half the other side of Myrtletown Hotel
about 400 yds from the main road I was pointed out the body

of a man by a little girl called Katie Damrow. The body was lying on its left side behind a log. The right arm was bent. The hand resting on the ground was grasping a small revolver. In the right breast pocket I found a pocketbook which contained a letter addressed to Dr Hirschfeld. When I found the body the hair on his beard was slightly singed.

The stone cast up into the air comes down to earth.
Again and again your son will return
to you, my land,
I am yours in great anger and defection,
in unfaithfulness . . . I am tossed away a hundred times . . .

Dear Romola, remember, in the days we leapt through
the Renaissance together, you on my shoulders, 'I will be
the new Vasari', you shouted. I know what you meant,
sweet hoarder of people and gossip and the old law
that hides itself in songs of paint and compulsion.
Be tolerant, little Vasari.
Only those tempted can know how easily virtue rests
on untried wooden pillars. On those damp logs
innocence glows phosphorous as fungus. I write
from a place of stilts. There are many growths:
I no longer differentiate corruption. Innocence
can look with monstrous padlocks.
Stork, stork, why are your feet bleeding?
That bird flew high, above enclosed orchards —
a deer leapt across the wall — fruit hung freely —
each thicket was figtrees. The stork was tempted
utterly.
          Romola, your mother will be
at the theatre, applause in her hair and a new lover.
You will not be alone, you are plotting
testimony.

Katie Damrow on oath saith:
   I am a single girl I reside with my parents at Myrtletown on the day I was gathering wood in the bush I know Mr Logan's

house near that house I saw the dead body I was frightened so
I got into my cart and drove home I told my father

The stone cast into the air clicks back. Toss it.
Budapest parts my flesh, the white stag
invents its thousand candle thorns.
Your mother's a jewelled snake.
In my hidingplace I wish you songs.
Some lands are strange,
some have no appetite
they harbour bitter figs.

Eugen Hirschfeld on oath saith:
I went to the hospital morgue with the German Consul. We
identified Charles Pulszky whom we knew. I had known him
about two months: he was that time in the colony. He was a canvasser at the time of his death. He had no relatives in the colony.
His father was an officer in the Austrian Army. Deceased had
been married – his wife is Emilia Markus, an actress celebrated
in Hungary. Deceased has two children, one fifteen years, one
about eight. I do not know why deceased committed suicide.

First sign: hills above Brisbane.
This land has no deer.
At that call my neck snapped.
                          They shrugged, the others.
Marsh waters, the wind angry across swamp, there must be
flat space, grassland. My stag
opens two thousand years. Love I will cover your body
with my shroud   *grassland   I have daughters in Budapest*
ambitious
I have snakes drinking at my eyes
this is a calm time, today I am selling Life.

                          My friends explained:
there is game here, above Brisbane. Red deer
released as gift from the Queen in Balmoral.
The great and terrible myths follow us everywhere.

166

Fingers are pebbles, worn smooth.

Brisbane will crouch in its time.

Emmy, Emilia you see what is done, your Charlie
who believed everything has one last armlet
he forces himself free

let the girl toss nights, there is no father.
Give her dreams, then.
Not the end of the world, but across the curve.

My passport tells lies: its term is one year.
Not so long.
Take back my name father, I do not need yours now.

Antlers, the law, your blindness laughs
I guide you to the place.
My new grown antlers strike home
will you be hurt will you hurt
without words now?
With me it was the neck.
Why do your feet bleed?
I have found the place.

Get up father, get up mother,
The Ancient Ones have come.
They are the Old Law, they hide
in songs.

James Proud on oath saith:
    I made a search of the body.
    I found a revolver, one chamber discharged.
    I also found a chamois revolver case,
    a pair of kid gloves,
    a pocketbook, watch, a pair of eyeglasses,
    a snake jewelled armlet,
    a pair of sleeve links and six pence in silver,
    two boxes of matches, a linen handkerchief.

Acknowledgements

To the Literature Board of the Australia Council, for a senior writing fellowship and a special projects grant to complete the manuscript; to Adelaide University and to the Darling Downs Institute of Advanced Education, Toowoomba, Queensland for writer-in-residence terms during which much of the book was drafted; to Professor Ken Goodwin, Dr Bruce Dawe, David Malouf, Judith Rodriquez and Elizabeth Jolley for individual advice. To Mr Stan Prior of Myrtletown for local history and background material.

To Mrs Katalin Forrai and Dr Mihaly Cenner of Budapest for research assistance central to the undertaking of the project; also to Miss Gabriella Szabo-Páp of the Hungarian Ministry of Education and Culture, interpreter Miss Agnes Forro and her friends, and Zoltan Hálasz of the *New Hungarian Quarterly* for cooperation, advice and assistance.

To Mrs Tamara Nijinsky-Weninger, of Arizona, U.S.A. for supplying copies of personal family letters and advice regarding other material. To Mr Joszef Halmos for Kyra Nijinsky material.

To Dr Egon Kunz of Canberra for initial encouragement and to Mrs Edith Banki of Sydney, especially, for translating an enormous amount of Hungarian language material, including difficult and laborious legal and parliamentary documents.

To the National Széchény Library, Budapest for assistance in obtaining and copying research material, and to the Fryer Library, University of Queensland, Barr Smith Library, University of Adelaide, State Libraries of Victoria, New South Wales, South Australia and Queensland, and the Queensland State Archives and Oxley Library and *Courier Mail* Archives, Brisbane.

Acknowledgement is also made to the following for publication of excerpts from the work while in progress: *Arvon Foundation 1980 Anthology* (England), *The Camrose Review* (Canada), the *Age* (Melbourne), *Overland* (Australia) and *Poetry Australia*; and to the Australian Broadcasting Commission for the broadcast of a radio feature based on some of the material.

Also to the following for permission to use extracts: Penguin Books Ltd (London) for the Ferenc Juhász poem 'The Boy

Changed into a Stag Clamours at the Gate of Secrets'; to William Aspenwall Bradley for material from Misia Sert; to Thames and Hudson Ltd for the Kurt Blaukoff material from *Mahler: A Documentary Study*; to Macmillan Publishing Co. Inc. (New York) for the Vera Krasovskaya material from *Nijinsky*; to Eric Glass for the Romola Nijinsky material from *The Diary of Vaslav Nijinsky* and *Nijinsky*.

Agghazy, Maria G., *Italian and Spanish Sculpture*, Corvina Press, Budapest, n.d.

Bacher, Béla, *The National Fine Arts Museum 1906-1956*, Corvina Press, Budapest, 1956

Blaukopf, Kurt, *Mahler: A Documentary Study*, Thames & Hudson, London, 1976

Bodolai, Zoltan, *The Timeless Nation*, Hungaria Publishing Co., Sydney, 1978

Buckle, Richard, *Diaghilev*, Atheneum, New York, 1979

Buckley, Richard, *Nijinsky*, Weidenfeld & Nicolson, London, 1980

Cenner, Mihaly, *Emilia Markus*, Könyvébél, Budapest, 1962

Eliot, George, *Romola*, Penguin, Harmondsworth, Middlesex, 1980

Gold, A. & R. Fizcale, *Misia*, Macmillan, London, 1980

Juhász, Ferenc and Sándor Weöres, *Selected Poems* (Juhász translated by David Wevill), Penguin, Harmondsworth, Middlesex, 1970

Kabdebo, Thomas, *Diplomat in Exile: Francis Pulszky's Political Activities in England, 1849-1860*, East European Quarterly, New York, 1979

Krasovskaya, Vera, *Nijinsky*, Schirmer Books (Macmillan), New York, 1979

Lewis, David L., *Prisoners of Honour: The Dreyfus Affair*, Cassell, London, 1973

Mojzer, Miklós, *Dutch Genre Paintings*, Corvina Press, Budapest, 1867

Nijinsky, Romola (ed.), *The Diary of Vaslav Nijinsky*, Simon & Schuster (New York) and Victor Gollancz (London), 1936

Nijinsky, Romola, *Nijinsky*, Victor Gollanz, London, 1980

Painter, George C., *Marcel Proust: A Biography*, Chatto & Windus, London, 1966

171

Pulszky, Ferenc, *Eletem és Kovom* (*My Life and Times*), Szépirodalmi Könyvkiado, Budapest, 1890 (1958)

Pulszky, Francis and Theresa, *Memoirs of a Hungarian Lady*, vol. 1, Henry Colburn, London, 1850

Pulszky, Francis and Theresa, *Tales and Traditions of Hungary*, vol. 1, Henry Colburn, London, 1851

Pulszky, Francis and Theresa, *White, Red, Black: Sketches of Society in the United States during the Visit of their Guest*, Trübner and Co., London, 1853

Rajeczky, Benjamin (ed.), *Hungarian Folk Music*, UNESCO, Budapest, n.d.

Rambert, Marie, *Quicksilver*, Macmillan, London, 1975

Vasari, Giorgio, *Lives of the Artists* (translated by George Bull), Penguin, Harmondsworth, Middlesex, 1965